Everything to Gain

Also from the Carter Collection

The Blood of Abraham: Insights into the Middle East, by Jimmy Carter
First Lady from Plains, by Rosalynn Carter
Keeping Faith: Memoirs of a President, by Jimmy Carter
An Outdoor Journal, by Jimmy Carter

Everything to Gain

Making the Most of the Rest of Your Life

Revised Edition

Jimmy and Rosalynn Carter

THE UNIVERSITY OF ARKANSAS PRESS
FAYETTEVILLE 1995

Reprinted by arrangement with Random House, Inc., New York and Toronto.
The University of Arkansas Press paperback edition published 1995
All rights reserved
Manufactured in the United States of America

07   06   05   04   03   7   6   5   4   3

Designed by John Coghlan

☺ The paper used in this publication meets the minimum requirements of the American
National Standard for Permanence of Paper for Printed Library Materials Z39.48.1984.

Library of Congress Cataloging-in-Publication Data

Carter, Jimmy, 1924-
    Everything to gain : making the most of the rest of your life /
Jimmy and Rosalynn Carter. —University of Arkansas Press pbk. ed.
        p.   cm.
    Originally published: New York : Random House, c1987. With
amendments to cover a few changed circumstances.
    ISBN 1-55728-388-5 (alk. paper)
    1.Carter, Jimmy, 1924- —Philosophy. 2. Carter, Rosalynn—
Philosophy. 3. Life skills—United States. 4. Conduct of life.
5. Presidents—United States—Biography. 6. Presidents' spouses—
United States—Biography. 7. Emory University. Carter Center.
I. Carter, Rosalynn. II. Title.
E873.2.C375   1995
973.926'0922—dc20
    [B]   95-24257
                                                  CIP

For Jack, Chip, Jeff, and Amy

Acknowledgments

It was not easy for us to resurrect for public examination in this book some of the most traumatic experiences of our lives. A more natural inclination was to bury such events, and then go on to other matters that are more pleasant and less subjective. Our original plan was just to report the results of a health conference at the Carter Center, and to let our readers know about the personal habits that can add as much as eleven years to their life span.

However, in discussions with our Random House editor, Peter Osnos, we were encouraged to write with a wider scope—to retain, in a briefer form, the report on the health conference but to be much more personal and to include some thoughts on how to make the most of the rest of our lives. He helped us to avoid too much preaching, and to use the experiences of our own family and friends to illustrate the challenges and achievements, as well as the problems and failures, that most of us have to expect. We have needed a lot of assistance in writing this book, and Peter has served as editor, adviser, and sometimes as referee.

Achsah Nesmith did a lot of research and gave us many good ideas, using her experience as a news reporter, and joined Peter Osnos and us in the final stages of editing. As a longtime friend and White House speech writer, her assistance was invaluable.

Dr. William Foege and his medical associates at the Centers for Disease Control provided most of the facts about health care, and they have tried to ensure that the information we have given is accurate.

We are grateful to all of them, and also to the people whose own inspirational lives we have used as models. We did all the writing, and made the final decisions about both the contents and the wording, so any errors or omissions are ours.

Contents

Introduction

We live in such a remarkable time that it is difficult for us to comprehend the changes that have taken place in our lifetimes—and in our lifestyles—since we were both children in Plains, Georgia, in the 1930s. Every day the average life expectancy of Americans increases by seven hours—two days each week, twenty-five years in this century. We have seen our workday shrink greatly and retirement years come much earlier. According to a recent report, a third of all American men over the age of fifty-five no longer work! Only a generation or two ago our forebears labored through a lifetime to reach an exhausted old age, whereas we can look forward to a full, robust "second" life in our later years. It is possible to have an entirely different career after our first one has ended and even to weave two or three exciting vocations together, while our ancestors were lucky to survive into what we now think of as middle age.

This is a book primarily about how these changes and the opportunities they represent have affected us and our immediate family. It is also a book that we hope anyone will find helpful, a source of ideas and of reassurance. At different times in our lives we have voluntarily made some radical changes, moving from the U.S. Navy to a small family business, then into local, state, and national politics. We have also had to accommodate some involuntary changes, the most traumatic of which was leaving the White House in 1981. Although a complete departure from anything we have done before, our present work in all its variety is giving us a full and stimulating life.

· Political life has provided our family with both some very good times and complicated problems of an intensely personal nature. But our reaction to these experiences, we believe, has been similar to that of many people who have faced challenges of various kinds in their lives. We have dealt with unexpected deaths, with the frustration of carefully calculated hopes, and with the excitement of ideas born not only in moments of inspiration but, on occasion, from disappointment or anger. Our successes have enabled us to pursue many additional areas of interest; our unexpected failures have closed off avenues of service. In both situations, we have had to stretch our minds and hearts to encompass new realities. Above all, we have found that advancing age has not restricted us, but has actually let us go on experimenting, learning, and also teaching.

The way we have coped with life's ups and downs has been shaped by a multitude of factors from our early lives, our relationships, religious beliefs, and our stable home community. Wherever possible in this book we have tried to relate our experiences and reactions to those of other people we know or know about. Life in a governor's mansion or the White House is far from typical; therefore, we have used our life in Plains as the baseline from which we have measured our own shifting situation and the changes around us.

This is a book we both very much wanted to write, but it has not been easy for us to do together. We have completely different writing styles and work habits, and surprisingly often we have found we did not feel the same way about an event or had conflicting recollections about what actually took place. There was a dilemma: How could we write in the first person plural (using "we" and "us") when some of the events had been experienced by only one of us—or when we disagreed about what ought to be written? We finally resolved this problem by separating our individual comments and identifying their source by inserting our names. This solution allowed for clarifying differences of opinion and helped to eliminate any threat to the stability of our marriage.

We begin by describing the profound disappointment and frustration over our defeat in the presidential election of 1980. We returned home to Plains almost three months after Election Day, and faced additional personal crises involving our home life, our health, our personal finances, and the need to carve out new careers that would best allow us to use our talents. Jimmy was fifty-six; Rosalynn was fifty-three. We were no longer young, but we were definitely not old.

Like so many other people, we wanted to know how to preserve our good health in ways that would make our remaining years active and productive. That was our starting point for examining the changes that have occurred just since the time we were children—not only in the length of Americans' lives but in our style of living, a style possible today because there is so much less fear of crippling disease and early death than there used to be.

To a great extent this book deals with health—emotional and spiritual as well as physical. What can each of us do to protect our health, to live more years and to have more life in each year? What problems or priorities help or hinder us toward our goals? How are our habits shaped by our families? our religion? our background? How do we best prepare for leaving the rough-and-tumble "real" world of business or politics?

Working with some of the world's most knowledgeable health experts, we sponsored a comprehensive study of these questions, the results of which we will discuss in this book. We wanted to learn how to use available medical information to extend the life span of Americans and were surprised at much of what we discovered. It was startling to find that a person can lose as many as a dozen years of potential life by adhering to certain habits. We had never realized how much control we actually have over how long we might live. You will see that some of the answers in our study are very simple, perhaps even obvious. But knowledge of the obvious is not always easy to put into practice.

We will also look at the almost unlimited ways to expand the range of activity of our later years not only close to our home but in the larger world, and tell some inspirational stories about modern-day heroes. We have been involved directly in projects with some of them for a number of years and have recently become acquainted with the work of others. Few of these remarkable people are well known, but they provide models of achievement that make us want to imitate what they are doing to make our own lives even more fulfilling. For instance, through our involvement with Habitat for Humanity, an organization based in Americus, Georgia, that provides housing for people who need it all over the world, we have understood that any well-meaning person willing to work can make a difference.

We have been fortunate in being able to do a lot of overseas travel and have described here some of our experiences abroad. Such adventures are possible for almost anyone. The challenge lies in figuring out how to combine further education with the pleasures of traveling in distant places, and, on occasion, helping to make the lives of the people you visit a little better.

To illustrate some of the points we want to make in this book, we have included the down-home wisdom of Jimmy Townsend, a philosopher and writer from the north Georgia mountains. He is one of the friends we've made in recent years who, with their insight into human nature, have helped ease the painful transition to a new life.

So now, completing three score years (and a bit more), we are still looking for ways to make the most of the rest of our lives. What follows is what we have found—so far.

May 1995

An examination by the authors has revealed a few changed circumstances since this book was first published, and we have made appropriate amendments in the text. A notable exception is in describing the work of The Carter Center, especially in the areas of disease eradication, mental health, and conflict resolution. Our projects have expanded to such an extent that the revisions would be quite voluminous and would provide a different context for the other basic themes.

Eight years later, our lives are still as full of adventure and pleasure as ever. Now that we have nine grandchildren, this is, perhaps, an understatement.

Starting Over

*Experience is what you've got plenty of when you're no longer able to
hold the job.*

—Jimmy Townsend

We were back in Plains, where it had all begun. We stayed close,
both physically and emotionally, as we tried to help each other through
some difficult moments and become reacquainted with the only home
we had ever owned. Ours was a quiet bungalow nestled in a hickory
and oak grove just on the western boundary of our little town, a house
built in 1961, following three successive profitable years for Carter's
Warehouse. It had seemed quite spacious then, but its small rooms were
now crammed with our longtime possessions and hundreds of other
mementos of an abruptly terminated political career. On this cold
January day, however, both we and the house seemed strangely empty.

The first few days after we left the White House had been an exten-
sion of our previous life: after an uproarious welcome home, Jimmy
immediately went on an emotional trip to Wiesbaden, West Germany,
to welcome the American hostages back to freedom after their long
captivity in Iran.

JIMMY

Although I had not been to bed for three days during the final negotiations about the hostages, I didn't even feel the fatigue during our

long trip to Germany. But I returned to Plains completely exhausted, slept for almost twenty-four hours, and then awoke to an altogether new, unwanted, and potentially empty life.

Rosalynn and I were alone; our large official retinue of White House staff members and political associates were traveling back to Washington or to their former homes. It was deeply discouraging for me to contemplate the unpredictable years ahead.

Only later would we realize that many people have to accept the same shocking changes in their lives as we did that winter: the involuntary end of a career and an uncertain future; the realization that "retirement" age is approaching; the return to a home without the children we had raised there; new family relationships, for which there had been no preparation. And in our case, all this was exacerbated by the embarrassment about what was to us an incomprehensible political defeat and also by some serious financial problems that we had been reluctant to confront.

We fully acknowledged the special blessings that we had enjoyed in our lives until then, but this did not help much to alleviate the pain and doubts of the present moment. Now it would be necessary to make a difficult transition back to a private and perhaps even lonely existence, to assess more calmly what had happened to us, to take stock of our own strengths and resources, and eventually to build a new life within the bounds of what we thought would be both appropriate and fulfilling for a former First Family of the United States. This regression from the White House to an acceptable life in Plains, Georgia, would require attitudes and talents different from those we had used in our aggressive and successful struggle from obscurity to the achievement of our political goals.

It had been quite a journey: to the State Senate and then to the governor's mansion, to the far corners of the country during the presidential campaign, and finally to the White House. Now it was over—too soon, we thought. But it was over, and decisions had to be made about what we would do with the rest of our lives.

ROSALYNN

Once when we came home from the governor's mansion after having been there for almost a year, we went to the peanut warehouse and visited with Billy and some of our farmer customers; we walked up and down Main Street going in and out of the stores speaking to everyone; then we drove to the farms and walked over the fields and in the woods.

That evening I was in the kitchen cooking supper, and Jimmy was in the den. He called me: "Rosalynn, come in here for a minute." I went to see what he wanted. He had taken off his boots and was lying on the couch. "Sit down," he said, motioning beside him. I sat down. "When my term as governor is up and we come home to Plains to live, what are we going to do the second day?"

At the time we laughed—with three years still ahead of us in the governor's mansion. Now it was no laughing matter.

Our house had not been lived in for ten years, while we campaigned and spent time in the governor's mansion and the White House, and it needed a lot of work. Upkeep of the grounds had meant just raking off the fallen leaves early each winter. This had removed protection for the topsoil, which, along with the lawn, had washed away. We had never gotten around to putting a floor in our attic, and there was little space for storing the clothes, photographs, books, files, and other items that we had collected over the years. Now the boxes and crates we had brought home were stacked to the ceiling in the house and garage. And we could no longer merely mention a need to servants or someone in charge of buildings and grounds; we would have to do the work ourselves. As far as physical activity was concerned, we had enough to keep us busy for some time.

The mental challenge, however, was a different matter. Our most pressing thoughts were still about the past; it was not yet possible to envision a full and pleasant life during the coming years. Even though it had been almost three months since the election and we had had time to brood and plan and wonder about what the future held for us, we still had not made any final judgments. We had a few unavoidable obligations, but more ambitious options had not been explored. Uncharacteristically, we had decided to postpone any serious decisions, because we understood the need to pause for a while, to come to terms with our circumstances. It had not always been that way, at least not for Rosalynn.

ROSALYNN

In the early weeks after the election, while we were still in the White House, I had been angry, sad, anxious, and worried. Jimmy was stronger. He has always had the ability to let go, even when the worst that could happen does happen, and to turn his mind to the next step. I envy and depend on that trait in his character, even though it may add to my frustration at the moment. In the weeks and months after the 1980 election, there were times when I felt he was keeping up a brave front not only for the sake of the country but also for the comfort of our family. I would almost have preferred some private wailing and gnashing of teeth. When one or another of our family lashed out at the press, at the opponent, or occasionally at the voters, Jimmy would listen and say, "Well, did we do the best we could?" Yes, we had done the best we could, and not only that, we had done a good job. "Then," he'd reply, "what else could we have done?"

JIMMY

Although I have deep feelings about people and events and am not reluctant to weep openly when I am moved, I have always believed that it is a sign of weakness to show emotion by giving in publicly to despair, frustration, or disappointment. Instead of yielding to these pressures, I try to hide my own feelings, to reassure others by emphasizing the positive aspects of the situation, and to pray for strength and wisdom. Privately, I commit myself to overcoming the obstacles or to figuring out a new course of action. This is what I had to do following the election in 1980.

Although my disappointment was great, I kept it bottled up for a long time. Slowly, it began to ease as new challenges presented themselves that needed to be met. Right after the defeat, I tried to think of everything we could possibly accomplish during the few months left in the White House, and arranged the list according to feasibility, setting an ambitious schedule for myself and those around me. It was not easy to scale down my wish list from great and challenging dreams—such as bringing peace to the Middle East, ridding the world of nuclear weapons, and ensuring the human rights of all peoples everywhere—to those things that were possible in the time left. We had a heavy legislative agenda, and getting the hostages home was a pressing priority.

During rare moments of solitude in those first few days I reviewed events of recent months to see if we could have done anything differently and changed the results of the election. It seemed to me that short of bringing the hostages home in a dramatic triumph just before voting day, there was no way we could have overcome the political damage caused by their extended kidnapping. The whole nation was obsessed with our failure to secure their release—and so was I. I was doing everything I could, exploring every possibility to obtain freedom for the Americans without creating a bloodbath in Iran, which would surely have resulted in their death.

Once I was convinced, correctly or not, that we had done our best, then it was easier to accept the judgment of the voters and move on to other things. Rosalynn was not able to do this. She went about her official duties with her chin up, but she found it impossible to accept the result of the election. Over and over she would raise the same questions: "How could the press have been so bad?" "Why didn't the people understand our goals and accomplishments?" "How could God have let this happen?" Although some of the same questions pressed on me, I did not—or could not—express them, and spent a lot of our private time attempting to reassure her. My arguments and explanations didn't help much. The only thing that sustained her was the hope and expectation that I would run again for president and be elected. She found very little support for this from me or the rest of our family.

I have to admit to a lot of somewhat artificial cheerfulness during those early weeks. The more Rosalynn was upset, the more I tried to find ways to comfort her. I never admitted how deeply I was hurt and I still find it hard to do so. We had a few strained and unpleasant moments between us in those early weeks, and now I realize that with my calm and reassuring attitude it seemed to Rosalynn that I didn't recognize her pain.

We were both worried about what was going to happen to the country. When the voters decided to change horses in midstream, not only had they rejected us but almost 51 percent of them had chosen a horse determined to run back as fast as possible in the opposite direction. What about all the things we had wanted to do and thought we were going to have time to do? The list was long. We had worked hard and tried to do what was right and best for the country, and the job was far from done.

ROSALYNN

There was no way I could understand our defeat. It didn't seem fair that everything we had hoped for, all our plans and dreams for the country could have been gone when the votes were counted on Election Day. We had done all we could, and somehow it had not been enough. Events had mocked us. Jimmy said he had always heard that it was harder for a loving wife to accept anything that hurt her husband than it was for the husband to accept it, and I believe that to be true. I agreed that we had been given opportunities and achievements granted to very few, but I had to grieve over our loss before I could look to the future. Where could our lives possibly be as meaningful as they might have been in the White House?

The thing that helped keep me going in the final days of 1980 was that I was absolutely sure we would run again and win. Every time I mentioned that I could hardly wait, the family groaned collectively. But I was sure—and determined. No one in our family has ever given up easily, and I did not intend to do so now.

We didn't talk much in those early days about where we would go when we left Washington. Though this was a nagging concern in the back of our minds, we were busy with our routine duties and finishing up doing whatever we could in the little time left. We considered the future in bits and pieces rather than by working out a master plan. And although we had some ideas about what our retirement might be like, there was no way to imagine what would really happen. We could only wonder what would be best for us. We had thoughts about going back to Plains, our only real home, but neither of us knew whether that would work out. We worried that we might be bored and restless in a small town after the exciting life of the White House and the long years of political battles. One member of our family had no doubts about returning to Plains.

ROSALYNN

Amy came into our bedroom the night after the election and leaned over on our high-canopied bed with her head on her arms. "I'm sad about this election," she said. "We're all sad about the election, Amy, and we all worked and tried very hard to win," I answered. Her reply came back sharply, "Yes, but I don't want to go back to Plains to live. You may be from the country but I'm not. I've been raised in the city!" She was right. We had moved to the governor's mansion when she was just three years old. We told her we had not even discussed what we were going to do and that we might not even be going back to Plains. Maybe, we said, we would live in Atlanta.

To add to the pain of the election results and the uncertainties about the future, we had another serious setback. Before going to the White House, we had put all our financial affairs in a blind trust, and had carefully separated ourselves from these matters. In November, soon after the election, our financial trustee discussed with us what had happened to our estate during the four years we had been in the White House. The farmland had been rented, and Billy had been left in charge of the peanut warehouse operation. Now we learned that due to three years of drought in Georgia and several changes in the warehouse management, we were deeply in debt. The revelation came as a terrible shock. Even now it is uncomfortable for us to disclose this private matter, but it is a crucial part of the story.

After some unpleasant discussions about our family finances, we decided that the only chance to become solvent again would be to sell the entire warehouse operation and stop the high interest payments on outstanding loans before we also ran the risk of losing our farms and our house. It had not really occurred to us before this meeting that Plains might not continue to provide us with the financial base it always had. Just as almost two decades of political life were about to end we found that the results of the preceding twenty-three years of hard work, scrimping and saving, and plowing everything back into the business were now also gone. No one could accuse us of becoming rich in the White House. We had not expected to, but we had hoped at least to be able to leave with what we had had when we came in. That, too, was not to be. Now we really had no reason to go home to Plains.

As we struggled to recover from this unexpected financial blow, we decided to step back and count our blessings before we let the disappointments overwhelm us. On a cold day in November, about ten days after the election, we went out on the Truman Balcony to be alone. Our thoughts were tentative and unformed. With some luck, we agreed, we should still be able to save our home and farmland and regain our financial security. Perhaps we could write books, which might be successful, or think of some field of work that would be appropriate. We knew that at least one former president had made teaching college a career. In any case, we still had many assets, including our family. We had good health, a relatively youthful and vigorous outlook on life, and close friends; we had our religious faith to help us through the rough times. And most important, we had each other. As always, we knew we had the principal responsibility for shaping our own future.

We also found reassurance in the thought that our wildest dreams had been fulfilled when Jimmy achieved the presidency and that we had relished every day of our time in Washington. We were even able to laugh a little. Prime Minister Menachem Begin of Israel had just been to the White House for a long and characteristically thorny discussion about the peace process, and we agreed that it might be good to let the future president deal with him and the Middle East—along with inheriting Sam Donaldson and a few other truculent members of the White House press corps. There were a few positive things about losing the election.

Sitting there on the balcony, we reviewed our life up to that point—the excitement, the challenges, the successes, the never-to-be-forgotten experiences. It had been a good life. Our timing had been right in each of our ventures into politics, although on some occasions we didn't realize it until later. When Jimmy lost the governor's race in 1966, we thought our political world had come to an end. But as painful as it had been, if we had won that year we might never have made it to the White House. Looking back, we realized that that defeat was for the best. Lately, however, circumstances had certainly been working against us—with the explosion in oil prices, worldwide inflation, and, of course, the hostages being held interminably. But endings can be beginnings. Would we ever look back on this election and say losing was for the best?

ROSALYNN

> I was sure we would not. Even if we overcame the disappointment of the defeat and all our other problems and went on to make the most of our lives, I believed the country was surely going to suffer. The newly elected leaders had already made it clear that they didn't attach the same importance we did to peace, nuclear arms control, human rights, environmental quality—not even to education and mental health, which were very important to me.

It was less than a month after the election, in early December, when offers began to come in from publishers for us to write our memoirs, and they were welcome. Not only would the contracts help us repair our financial status but they would also keep us immersed in hard and unfamiliar work for a number of months while we dealt with our political disappointments and made plans for the future.

ROSALYNN

The days passed, and it was not long before the Christmas season came with all its activity at the White House. Official duties never cease at Christmastime, but the season is festive, sentimental, and fun. I have always loved Christmas and this one was no different. It was beautiful, and we were so caught up in it that we sometimes forgot to remember that this would be our last one in the White House.

When the holidays were over we turned our attention to entertaining friends for the last time. It was amazing how many people there were to thank. Night after night we had farewell parties, along with luncheons and receptions during the day. Except for a few rare periods alone, we still didn't have time to talk about the future, though as we stood in endless receiving lines we were sometimes reminded of it by well-meaning friends: "Don't you worry about the election. You're about to start on the most exciting part of your life." That was not true, it would never be true, and we'd rather not hear people say it. It took a lot of patience to smile sometimes. "We're glad you're going to be able to go home and get away from all the criticisms and the ugliness of politics." But we'd thrived even with the criticisms, and we loved politics. "I'm glad you're going to be out of here so you can have some peace and quiet for a change." But, of course, that was exactly what we were worried about! "Jimmy's just too good to be president." We appreciated our friends' concern, but there was just no way they could know how we were really feeling.

The last weeks in Washington were hectic. We found ourselves rushing to get everything done. We packed between parties and wrote thank-you notes. And the house was always full of company. Many close friends and relatives wanted to spend just one night in the White House while we were still there.

It's probably a good thing that Election Day comes early in November and Inauguration Day is not until late January. By then, acceptance, if not the understanding, of the voting results has come; bitterness subsides amid all the activity. And for us the negative mood was lightened by the good news of those last days: we had a remarkably successful lame-duck session with the Congress. Some of the Republicans who had opposed controversial legislation on Alaska lands, toxic waste, and energy conservation decided to lend their support so that their new president would not have to begin his term by dealing with these particular problems. And at the end we would even be able to bring the hostages home.

Although no specific words were ever spoken, as the days went by we all knew that when the time came we would go home—to Plains. We were ready to get on with the next part of our lives.

ROSALYNN

Now at home, we set about putting our house and yards in order. Jimmy's grandmother used to say she enjoyed being in "*my* house with *my* things," and, for a change, we knew how she felt. We didn't have to dress up every day for cameras. We'd still be working when the evening news came on, and most of the time we didn't stop to watch it! And for the first time in many years we were in charge of our own schedules.

When President Harry Truman was asked by a newsman what was the first thing he did after he got back home to Independence, he said, "I took the grips up to the attic." Now we needed to do that, but we couldn't since we had never gotten around to finishing the upper part of our house. So the first thing we did was put down a tongue-and-groove floor in the attic to provide some much-needed storage space. It was a difficult job, carrying all the long boards up a rickety folding ladder, working in the cramped spaces, chiseling and planing the uneven joists to provide a smoothly finished surface, notching out and fitting each board snugly around the ceiling braces and other obstructions, and nailing them in, often with little room to swing the hammer. It was hot and stuffy, but we didn't want anyone to help us. The hard work was good physical and mental therapy.

And we valued the time together. After years of involvement in important events and decisions, which necessarily meant separations, we again had time for true companionship. We shared memories about our times in the White House, some hilarious and some sad. We walked in the woods, jogged, rode bicycles on the rural roads around Plains, fished in our own pond, and went to bed at night physically exhausted.

ROSALYNN

One day we were working in the yard and we laughed when I commented that it seemed astounding that the most important thing in my life could be whether or not the brick walk we were building from our house to the street was crooked or straight. And it *was* very important!

Along with these more simple pleasures, there were responsibilities that we could not avoid. Working mostly from our home, we organized a small staff and volunteers to handle the voluminous mail that poured in. Correspondence and the telephone took a lot of time. To our vast relief, we soon negotiated the sale of our warehouse business to Archer-Daniel-Midland Company. We were able to ensure that the interests of our longtime employees were protected and that there was a reasonable prospect that the business would be cared for and expanded in the future. After all, the warehouse was an integral part of the Plains agricultural community and, we strongly felt, an asset to our town. The sales price was not a windfall, but we did receive just enough to pay off our debts and didn't have to sell any of our farmland. Also, by early summer we had both signed contracts to write our books, and being financially back on our feet lifted our spirits.

ROSALYNN

Our books would be entirely different. Jimmy planned a presidential memoir limited to our four years in Washington, while my story would be about growing up in a tiny south Georgia town, falling in love with my best friend's brother, and forming a partnership with him that led from a rural peanut warehouse to the White House.

When I began working on my book, Edmund Morris, one of the country's leading presidential biographers, said to me, "Don't try to make your place in history. It's already made." Suddenly I realized that I didn't have to "set the record straight" in some combative way as I had originally intended. The events were all there for everyone to see. I didn't have to write them all down. I was free to write my story, the story of my life, and so my book became an autobiography.

JIMMY

Soon after returning home, even before choosing a publisher, I began working on my book. For the first time I read the diary notes—six thousand pages of them—that I had dictated at least once a day while we were in Washington. Needless to say, this was not always enjoyable as I relived the events while marking and cataloging the more interesting entries that would provide a source for the book. But it gave me a chance to come to terms with the more unpleasant events and put them in perspective along with the important things we had been able to achieve. Aside from my diary, I had detailed information about every day of my life in the White House: a president's every move is recorded, every visitor is logged in and out, the telephone operators list each call that is placed or received, and every public word expressed verbally or in writing is recorded and published each week—even the offhand quips to news reporters while getting on or off the helicopters on flights to and from Andrews Air Force Base or Camp David. It was not difficult, therefore, to reconstruct what had taken place over the four years, with my diary providing the inside story. I was often surprised at the differences between the indisputable facts as recorded and my later recollection of them, and in retrospect I could see trends developing in an issue much earlier than was detectable at the time. I can vouch for the advantages of hindsight.

I also began making plans to realize a lifelong ambition. For years I had wanted to teach, ever since my days as a young naval officer helping enlisted men pursue their high school and college educations aboard a battleship. Now I would have my chance—although four years earlier than anticipated! Even before leaving the White House I had begun to receive offers from major universities to serve in both teaching and administrative positions. There was a precedent: William Howard Taft left the White House in 1913 and then taught law for a number of years at Yale University. After considering the possibilities, I decided to cast my lot with Emory University in Atlanta, a relatively small institution that was eager to improve its academic standing and influence. I was named a "distinguished professor," and began to lecture in the various colleges of the university as requested by senior professors and deans, and to add my perspective to classes in law, political science, history, international relations, medicine, logic, ethics, theology, anthropology, and business. My classes range in size from a half-dozen graduate students to a cross section of the student body in large town-meeting-style forums.

For at least the first few months there was one disagreeable prospect ahead of me that I tried to ignore: the need to raise large sums of money to build a presidential library for the records of my administration. I had never been a good fundraiser, even when I was the likely winner of an important political race. Now, a defeated Democrat with no desire to seek public office again, the thought of having to go hat in hand for cash contributions was disheartening, to say the least.

Not long after we came home we got two new word processors and enjoyed learning to use them. We both knew how to type, and although we had not done so for years, the skill came back and we enjoyed using our fascinating new machines. It is not an exaggeration to say that we were like children with new toys.

ROSALYNN

In an interview for the *New York Times,* Jimmy called his "my trusty word processor" as though it were a good friend. I felt the same way. Our love of the machines was an incentive for us to write every day. It is astounding how much this technical innovation became a factor in our adjustment to a new life.

Jimmy's study was in what had originally been our garage, and I made an office for myself out of one of our small bedrooms at the other end of the house. With his references ready at hand, Jimmy began writing immediately. My first task was to learn more about myself. I had long conversations with my mother and recorded them on tapes, which I will always cherish. I talked with my daddy's sister, who was ninety and the only living family member of their generation. My father had died when I was thirteen, and I learned much about him that I had never known. I talked with my brothers and sisters, my former classmates, and with older citizens in our community. Reliving my childhood and learning about my ancestors were pure enjoyment. I had so much information written down about the earlier period of my life that I didn't have room to include much of it in my book. For instance, I learned that my daddy's mother climbed out the window at age sixteen and eloped with a traveling salesman named Mr. Smith, who was crippled and twenty-five years older than she was. I'm saving these anecdotes for our grandchildren.

I found navy documents and newspaper clippings about our years at home. I had an entire scrapbook about Jimmy's first race for the State Senate, when the ballot box was stuffed against him and we had to go to court before Jimmy eventually won the election. I had my daily schedules from the governor's mansion. Edna Langford, who had campaigned with me for two years in the presidential election, had written a book about the campaign. We had stayed in people's homes, and she had called everyone we stayed with and gotten comments from them about what we did. I had all that material available in chronological order. And to increase the load of information, every move in the White House is documented not only for the president, but for members of his family. Along with daily schedules of appointments and visitors, there is even a log noting each time a member of the family goes upstairs or down from the second or third floors in the White House: "7:05 A.M. Mrs. Carter downstairs and to the Oval Office . . . 7:22 Mrs. Carter returns and goes upstairs"; and there is also a record of who ate every meal and what was served, and who slept in every bed every night!

Writing was a new experience for me, and for months I didn't let anyone read what I had written. (Jimmy didn't read my book until the first drafts were finished.) I was too embarrassed to share it, afraid of being laughed at. But I had to know if the book was good, bad, or somewhere in between. Our daughter-in-law, Judy, is a professional writer, so when she was visiting one day, I decided to let her read it. I trusted her judgment and knew she would tell me the truth. She took the material into another room and after a while came back into the den, where I was waiting nervously. "It's pretty good," she said. Pretty good! Those were some of the best words I had ever heard. I was thrilled and ready to go back to work.

One problem we had at the beginning was privacy. An extraordinary number of people came through Plains to look at our hometown, and many of them expected to visit with us. We enjoyed seeing them, but with several dozen each week, normal life was impossible. So we had an open house for everyone in Plains, including a large contingent of tourists, and when foreign visitors, such as President Sadat of Egypt, came to town, we invited as many guests as our house could accommodate. Otherwise, we insisted on some privacy. It wasn't as though we were in hiding. Our assistants could always tell visitors, "Well, you can come to Maranatha Baptist Church on Sunday morning. Both the president and his wife will be there, and they will be glad to see you."

We still found it increasingly difficult to write for very long without interruptions. Several times we commented wistfully about the serenity of Camp David, the presidential retreat in the Catoctin mountains. A perfect solution presented itself when our friends Betty and John Pope showed us a twenty-acre lot, alongside a cold, clear mountain stream, in north Georgia. We decided, together with them, to build a log cabin, and the place is everything we dreamed it would be—isolated, quiet, and beautiful, with a waterfall and small rapids in our front yard. It gives us a secluded place to write, think, and be together. It is a retreat in the best sense of the term.

JIMMY

Before we left Washington, my Cabinet and staff gave me a wonderful gift: a complete set of tools and machinery for a woodworking shop.

I had made furniture since I was a high school boy, but for the first time I was equipped to do many things that were not possible before. Now I was able to design and build the furniture for our new cabin. Just a few steps from the word processor, my woodshop gave me a chance to rest and clear my mind as I wrote the book. It was good therapy, too—especially when I was turned down by prospective donors for the presidential library or frustrated with recalling crises over OPEC, Iran, the press, or Congress—to be able to go to my shop and design, cut, fit, and finish a piece that was useful, permanent, and sometimes beautiful—or to just bang on something.

Gradually, as we recovered from the exhaustion of our last months in Washington and settled in at home, we began to feel that life in Plains might turn out to be satisfying. We became confident that we would find significant outside activities while living in the quiet environs of our youth. We especially enjoyed the luxury of walking through the woods and fields for miles without seeing a single house, or of rarely meeting a car while bicycling or jogging along the back roads. We would stop along the way to visit the farm families who had been our friends and customers before we left home for a political life, and we rapidly became reinvolved with them in the life of our community. We savored the different seasons of nature and gathered wild fruits, such as plums, blackberries, mayhaws, grapes, blueberries, and persimmons that grow along or near the rural trails. We planted a garden our first year and struggled to can, dry, or freeze the almost inexhaustible supply of vegetables that we harvested ourselves. And having our mothers close by to call or visit every day was a particular joy.

What we had done was to seek out, in our chosen home community, those things that were the most meaningful to us. We realized that it is all too easy to ignore the natural beauty and simple pleasures right around us and to complain instead about dull surroundings or the inevitable hard knocks of life.

As nowhere else could ever be, Plains was the place where we could be the same couple we had been before the White House years, doing such things as arranging the flowers at church when it was our turn and teaching Sunday School. Here in all the world were people who loved us for ourselves and not for whatever power or influence we might have had, who had known our names when the rest of the world still said "Jimmy Who?" and remembered our fathers and still cared about our mothers just as they would have if we had remained peanut farmers.

But these healing days were not without their relapses.

ROSALYNN

I had learned many years ago to release my problems to God, something I had to do often in all our political years when I was trying to do so many different things at once. "Here it is, God. You take it. I can't handle it alone," I would say. It helped me through the good times and the bad. I knew that God loved me. I had found God's love a shield around me that protected me in the midst of controversy or letdowns. Sometimes now, when I thought about the defeat and how much I disagreed with what our successor was doing in Washington, I was having to say, "It's too much for me. Here it is again, God. Take it again." And on occasion when I was tired, or when I read or heard a particularly disturbing negative news story about us, or learned, for instance, that all the funding for our mental health legislation was being cut, or when I saw Amy so hurt by her transition home, it was hard to give it to God.

One day soon after we came home, my brother Murray, who was a teacher at Amy's school, called us to say, "You ought to get Amy to bring somebody home with her and make some real friends. All the girls in her class are planning a camping trip this weekend. They talk about it in the classroom and in the lunchroom and during play period, and they haven't asked Amy to go with them."

We didn't mention it to Amy that night, deciding to give her another day to bring it up herself. The next night Murray called again. "That's all right about Amy. I found out why they haven't invited her. They don't want those guards [Secret Service agents] watching them all weekend long."

We were relieved a few days later when Amy came home from school and said, "I'm going to be late getting home Monday, because I've been invited to a birthday party after school." On Monday she came home at the regular time. "What happened to the party, Amy?" "Well, Mary came to school this morning and said her mother decided if I wanted some cake she would have to bring it to me because she wasn't going to feed all those policemen!" That night when we called her to dinner and she didn't come, we found her outside in a tree, crying.

Rosalynn

"I don't understand it. I just don't understand why God wanted us to lose the election," I would say. Jimmy was always more mature in his Christian attitude than I was. He would say, "Do you think people are robots that God controls from heaven?"—or "You don't really think God orders things like this, do you? It's hard for us to accept the fact that our priorities are not the same as God's. We attach too much importance to things like popularity, wealth, and political success. To Him problems that often seem most important to us at the time are really not very significant. But God trusts us to make the best use of the time we have, to try to live like Jesus and to make our lives meaningful and beneficial to others no matter where we are." I did finally learn to live with the results of the 1980 election, but I would never pretend that it came easily.

Not long after we came home, Amy went off to boarding school in Atlanta, our last child to leave home. We were lonely without her, and we tried to do our afternoon jogging or bicycling at the time she used to come home from school so that we wouldn't subconsciously wait for her return. We missed her terribly, but there was no doubt that it had been time to let her go.

Amy had not been happy at home. She was heartbroken when we left Washington; leaving all your friends at age thirteen is not easy. There were only two people her age in Plains and they went to a different school, so she hardly knew them. Most of her classmates lived in another county where her school was located. After she went off to Atlanta's Woodward Academy, she started to make new friends; the work was challenging, and she was soon involved in many extracurricular activities. One day a few months later when someone mentioned the election and we heard Amy say, "Yeah, but if Dad had won, I wouldn't know my friends at Woodward," we knew that Amy's healing process was well under way, too.

There was another adjustment that we had to make. For the first time we were both at home together all day every day, and as much as we care for each other this sometimes proved difficult. We each had been accustomed to having some space of our own, some free time to be alone, to think and work independently—which, luckily, we both thought was important. Now, as the days passed, we had to learn to share time. Through trial and error, building upon our own inclinations and our knowledge of each other, we worked out an acceptable relationship. But it was still not easy, especially when we became immersed in writing our books.

ROSALYNN

Jimmy would get up very early in the morning, most often at 5:00 A.M., and work for several hours before breakfast. I'm not an early-morning person, and after I got up and joined him for breakfast at seven-thirty, I liked to take a bath leisurely and get ready for the rest of the day. Jimmy would leave the breakfast table and go back to work on his book, and inevitably by the time I sat down to get started on mine he was ready for a coffee break!

I was also trying to keep everyone from bothering him so he could write—isn't that an expected wifely duty?—which meant that I was answering the telephone, keeping any guests and family members away from him, and deciding what to have for lunch or dinner.

I started my own writing in April. One day in August when Judy was visiting I went into my office early in the morning and called up the current chapter on the word processor. With one interruption after another, by four o'clock in the afternoon I hadn't written one new sentence! I was so exasperated that I went into the backyard, slamming the door, and walked for a while. I picked up the water hose to water the flowers and shed a few tears while I worked through my frustration.

When I came back inside, Jimmy and Judy were waiting for me: "We're going to help you discipline yourself to get your book written." They made a sign that said, WORKING HOURS 9–12 A.M.—DO NOT DISTURB and put it on the door of my office. "Does this mean you, too?" I asked Jimmy. "Yes," he said.

It worked. And with the undisturbed hours in the morning that allowed me to become engrossed in my writing, I found I could work for the rest of the day even with some interruptions. My secretary stopped calling until the afternoon. Family members knew when to come to see me. It was wonderful. I could shut the door to my office and be alone. I could laugh out loud, I could cry. I even surprised myself with some of the things I could write. Sometimes I would call Judy and say, "Listen to this, I wrote it!" If I got tired, I could go outside and walk in the yard. Jimmy helped me have that time, too. My mind didn't stop working even though I was tired of sitting and typing, and I didn't like to break my train of thought. And sometimes I wanted a coffee break with him.

JIMMY

Never since childhood had I spent any working days around the house, so being at home was a strange experience for me. With the book to write, the plans to be developed for the library, and the need to raise funds for it, I never felt the aimlessness that might come with being so newly and suddenly retired. I was busy from the first day, and once I began to unwind and realize that for the rest of my life I could work on whatever I wanted—when I wanted—I began to relish the freedom. I agreed with Rosalynn on how important it was to learn to respect each other's privacy, to "do our own thing," but I came to depend on having a standing date for late afternoons, when we could relax together. Although I was distressed by some of the changes taking place in Washington, I usually managed to control my public criticisms and concentrate on my own work. There is no doubt that the healing period after the political defeat was also a learning process for both of us, sometimes together and at other times a slowly evolving understanding deep within us individually.

ROSALYNN

After having someone else prepare our meals for years, I enjoyed being in the kitchen again. I looked forward to taking a break from writing at lunch time and putting together a good soup or salad, or even cooking a gourmet dish. Jimmy is a good cook. He helped in the kitchen many years ago when the children were small and we all came home from the peanut warehouse in the evenings tired from a day's work. Now he enjoyed experimenting with new ways to cook quail or fish or other dishes, and our evening meal could be adventurous. But life was not yet idyllic.

After a few months of writing I had done the easier parts of my book and it was time to tackle the difficult ones.

I began to have aches and pains, which I thought came from sitting at the word processor day in and day out. My back hurt and my legs were stiff. When I got up from my chair I could hardly straighten up, as though I had been molded to fit it. I began to run a constant low-grade temperature. The pains got progressively worse, spreading to my neck and shoulders, and then all over. I had always been healthy and active, but now I had to give up my exercising. I started taking aspirin to ease the pain. The local doctor could find nothing wrong with me. I went to another, with the same result. But something was definitely wrong! I was still writing every day, though not for long periods of time without getting up and moving around.

I was determined not to give in to this mysterious affliction. When it kept getting worse, I finally went to a doctor at Emory University Clinic in Atlanta. He put me in the hospital, and I think I had every test there is. The results showed a thyroid deficiency that the doctors said could be controlled with medication. But there was no agreement on a precise diagnosis for my rheumatoid arthritis symptoms. There was, however, a consensus that I was suffering from polymyalgia rheumatica, an inflammation of the muscles. My doctor thought it best that I not take steroids to control the pain, and said that if I could treat it with anti-inflammatory drugs he was sure I could wear it out. I did wear it out, but it took a long time. It was maddening not to be able to do the things I had always done. My spirits suffered, and my book suffered.

After six or eight months when I had lost all flexibility, I knew I had to do something or I would never be able to move freely again. I got several exercise video tapes and tried to go through them. I finally settled on a Jane Fonda *Work-Out,* one I liked because so much of it involved the stretching that I needed. And though I couldn't possibly keep up with Jane or stretch half as much as I should have been able to, I kept at it every day when I got up in the morning, and slowly I began to be able to move more comfortably. I'm sure I was "wearing out the disease" as the doctor had said, but I am also sure that the exercises were partially responsible for my recovery.

I wondered then and still do now whether all the pent-up emotions from our defeat and our new circumstances could possibly have been the culprit for my illness. Though I thought I had come to terms with these pressures, had I just been forcing myself to put them out of my mind instead of dealing with them? As we've both already said, it had been hard losing the election, discovering that our business had failed, trying to carve out an entirely new life for which we had not made plans, acknowledging the anguish of our only daughter in moving away from her friends to a tiny village that she hardly knew, then seeing her—our last child at home—go off to boarding school, and to top it all, forcing myself to write a book about our highly personal experiences for the world to read. I had certainly accumulated my share of stress points, so maybe I shouldn't have been surprised when I began to develop pains. Jimmy had said that when he was writing he sometimes found it necessary to go out to his woodshop and bang on something. Maybe I should have been doing the same thing! I will never know for sure what happened to me, but I recovered. I guess the body, the mind, and the spirit are connected.

It was a proud day for me when I finished my book. I am one who wouldn't even let Jimmy read what I wrote in Christmas cards when we were first married. It had taken longer than I'd ever dreamed it would take—almost three years. Jimmy, who is more disciplined than

I, had finished his in a year. But I tease him. My book was number one on the *New York Times* best-seller list; he always had Jane Fonda's exercise book ahead of his. And mine was on the list for eighteen weeks; his was on for eleven! He takes my ribbing good-naturedly, however. His book sold more copies than mine, *but* reprint sales have still not been counted, and I'm going to beat him yet. Our friendly competition goes on.

Planning and dreaming about the presidential library had taken a lot of our time, almost from the day we came home. We had found the perfect site for it in the heart of Atlanta—thirty acres located between downtown and Emory University, only a short distance from each. It is an area that was cleared for a highway intersection in the early seventies, but the highway was never built. We felt very fortunate, except for the burden of raising the $25 million necessary for construction.

The special facilities that have to be designed and built for the proper storage of presidential records are a costly project—the "onerous responsibility of a former president," as can be attested to by at least two former presidents. Gerald Ford told us that his fund-raising effort was the worst job he had ever had in his life, and we can sympathize. While this mission was being accomplished, we were still pondering what the library should be, how it could be used. We certainly didn't want it to be a lifeless memorial.

ROSALYNN

Jimmy was already calling the museum area a "teaching center." He didn't want it to be simply a glorification of the political life and times of our family. He insisted, "I don't want a monument to me." Rather, he wanted it to be our gift to the people of our country in appreciation for receiving such a high political honor. We explained our thoughts to several architects, who drew up proposals and presented them to us.

The day of their presentations turned out to be very difficult for us. The plans were all impressive, but not what we wanted. One was like a temple, looming toward the sky, which, as the architect said, could be seen from anywhere in Atlanta. The main focus, the spire, was meant to represent the Camp David accords and contained from different perspectives a cross, a Star of David, and a Muslim crescent. We had invited a few friends to view the plans with us, and most of those present—including me—agreed that with some changes this one might be a good representation of the Carter presidency. The architect had very strong feelings about what Jimmy had accomplished, and wanted to say to the country and the world that his administration was good and honorable and stood for peace and human rights. But Jimmy was adamant in his opposition. He was so upset that I could see the vein in his temple throbbing. When he said he didn't want a monument, he clearly meant it more than I imagined.

After everyone left we couldn't even talk about it. The fact that I thought the plans had possibilities left no room for words. That night on the way to our mountain cabin, Jimmy said, "I'm not going to have a library." At the time he meant it.

After much deliberation and discussions with friends, one of them took the situation in hand. Realizing the problem we were having, Chris Hemmeter, a young developer from Hawaii, arrived in Plains one day with a new set of artist's drawings and a remarkable audio tape—complete with dramatic background music from *Man of La Mancha*—describing what the library could be. It really was beautiful; even Jimmy agreed. Soon a partnership was formed between one of the Atlanta architectural firms and a group from Hawaii, and detailed planning began.

Busy as we now were with our books and the library, there was still the longer-term question of how we could make our work more meaningful.

ROSALYNN

One night I woke up and Jimmy was sitting straight up in bed. He always sleeps so soundly that I thought he must be sick. "What's the matter?" I asked. "I know what we can do at the library," he said. "We can develop a place to help people who want to resolve disputes. There is no place like that now. If two countries really want to work something out, they don't want to go to the United Nations and get one hundred fifty other countries involved in the argument. I know how difficult it is for them to approach each other publicly, and they take a chance on being embarrassed by a rebuff from the other party. We could get good mediators that both sides would trust, and they could meet with no publicity, no fanfare, perhaps at times in total secrecy. If there had been such a place, I wouldn't have had to take Begin and Sadat to Camp David. There've been a lot of new theories on conflict resolution developed since that time, too, and we might put some of them into use." He talked on enthusiastically about other areas where negotiation might help—in domestic disputes and in dealing with civil laws. A center to settle disputes. For the first time since our return to Plains I saw Jimmy really excited about possible plans for the future.

A few days later we were in Hawaii on a fund-raising mission and presented our plans for the library to a group of young executives. Because of the five-hour time change, we awoke early in the morning and lay in bed discussing our future, pursuing eagerly the notion of a center at the library for resolving disputes, even if it had to be many years in the future. We agreed that we still had a lot to do to establish ourselves before that could happen. Writing, teaching, developing the presidential library, and managing the family farms seemed like a full enough agenda, but some of these tasks would soon be finished, and we both understood before daybreak that as much as we enjoyed being at home and having a "normal" life, there was still a crucial something missing: an opportunity for service that had been so much a factor in our political lives.

We talked for several hours into the morning about our interests, how much time we would have available, and what specifically we would like to work on if we had a chance and the right forum. We still had an intense concern with the issues we had faced in the White House: peace and nuclear arms control; human rights, including the alleviation of hunger and suffering among the world's poor; health care and adequate services for the mentally afflicted. Although we knew, of course, that some of these were the responsibilities of governments, we asked ourselves, Why not sponsor expert analyses, unrestrained discussions among leaders in a nonpartisan forum, and accurate reporting of facts to the public? We could be bold and set maximum challenges for ourselves. After all, we had done it before.

And so the idea of the Carter Presidential Center took shape. Between Emory University and the presidential library there would surely be ways to study, analyze, discuss, and maybe even take action on some of the issues that were important to us and to our country and the world.

JIMMY

"Who knows what we can do if we set our objectives high? We may even be able to do more than if we had won the election in 1980!"

We looked at each other and began to laugh. If we could begin to minimize the defeat, then we must be in good shape. We were happier that morning than we had ever been since we left the White House. We now had something tangible to work toward.

ROSALYNN

Once on the tour across the country to promote my book, a woman asked me in an interview, "Isn't it sad to see the president just out in his woodshop making little wooden objects with his hands?" If she only knew!

What we had come to realize as "retired" people is that we have a lot more leeway than ever before to choose our own path, to establish our own priorities. We had a lifetime of training and experiences on which to base these decisions, and our financial resources would be adequate to meet our needs. We had nothing to lose in whatever we did and everything to gain.

Allan Fromme says in his book, *Life after Work*, "It's not what you did. It's what you're doing." We had weathered a difficult passage. We had overcome the crisis of involuntary retirement and all the strains it placed on us. We had grown with the adversity, and we were closer than ever before. It had taken a long time. We had had to work our way through various stages—self-pity, anger, discouragement, anxiety. But after this period of sometimes painful readjustment, we had come to accept our new circumstances. Finally, we had made the exciting discovery that our lives do not need to be limited to past experiences. The future could be challenging and fulfilling as well.

There is life after the White House!

Closing the Gap

*Health nuts are going to feel real stupid someday—lying in hospitals,
dying of nothing.*

—Redd Foxx, the comedian

ROSALYNN

Late one summer afternoon Jimmy and I rode bicycles out of town to
one of our farms to look at the crops. It was also the season for blackberries, and we thought we would gather some for breakfast next
morning.

As we walked over the fields we came to the small cemetery where
my ancestors are buried. This farm has been in our family since my
great-great-grandfather drew the original land lots and settled here in
the 1830s. The birth dates on some of the grave markers stretch back
to the 1700s. We noticed that few of these early settlers had reached
what we would now call a "ripe old age." Several had died within a
period of a few weeks, and I remembered my mother telling me that
dysentery had taken their lives. There was the grave of a sixteen-year-
old girl who had died from burns when her clothes caught fire as she
stood before an open fireplace. And it was particularly sad to see the
number of tiny graves of infants, and to think of how many children in
those days had died at childbirth or in the first months of life.

We thought about our own children and grandchildren and about how fortunate we are to live in an age when we know so much more about health care than our ancestors did. Infectious diseases were the main causes of death in the days of poor sanitation, unpasteurized milk, contaminated drinking water, and the lack of refrigeration. And when someone contracted a contagious disease, such as typhoid fever or influenza, it would sweep through a family and sometimes an entire community. Even minor injuries often resulted in death from infection. Fear was part of the fabric of life in a way we cannot imagine, but which is still felt today by parents in many developing countries—countries, incidentally, where 90 percent of the world's population live.

Since those early days, our life spans have increased dramatically because of the removal of many unsanitary health hazards and the widespread use of immunizations and wonder drugs.

Until recently, life expectancy was not something we thought much about in terms of our own lives. We were young and active enough to consider the effects of advancing age only as they applied to other people. But, naturally, as we grow older the subject of how long and how well we can expect to live becomes one of increasing interest. Standing there, in the cemetery, being reminded of how much illness dominated the short lives of our ancestors, we were struck with the extent to which we have tended to take good health for granted. Even in our lifetime, conditions have dramatically changed from what we remember as children—more, perhaps, than in any other period of human history.

So as we began to see the Carter Center as a place to pursue work on important issues, we decided that one of our highest priorities should be the further prevention of unnecessary sickness and premature death at home and around the world.

JIMMY

This had been a long-standing concern for me, dating back to my early childhood experiences: My mother nursed actively when I was growing up and most of her close circle of friends were doctors and nurses. The suffering of those in our community was an everyday topic of conversation in our household.

As governor and then as president I had a special interest in preventive health care. One of my initiatives in Georgia was a comprehensive study of the major cripplers and killers of our people so that we could take the steps necessary to prevent them. The same sort of project was a priority for me as president, and a definitive analysis of our nation's health resulted in Surgeon General Julius Richmond's 1979 report, entitled *Healthy People*. It is still a seminal volume on the subject. Another important program during the presidential years was the inoculation of all American children against contagious diseases.

Rosalynn has always shared my concern about health issues and has been a leader in improving mental health programs at the state and national level. And when I was president, it was she who approached the secretary of health, education, and welfare (now HHS) about the immunization program for the children in the country.

ROSALYNN

We set a goal of immunizing 90 percent of the nation's children against measles over a two-year period, 1977–79. By the time Jimmy left office we were close to eliminating measles from the United States. A side effect of this effort, federal health officials say, was a decline in other serious childhood diseases, including mumps, rubella, diphtheria, and tetanus. The key then—and today—was getting parents to take their children to a clinic or a doctor for measles vaccination, because once they were there they received other immunizations as well.

Most of us get our health information in bits and pieces: the results of a new study somewhere are reported in the news; we hear some celebrity explain her ice cream diet or exercise regime; someone on a talk show, who claims to know, says we should never have calcium and iron at the same meal or should eat bean curd six times a day. After a while we get confused, conclude that "everything gives you cancer or is fattening," and decide to forget the whole business of improved nutrition or exercise because we don't know whom or what to believe or how it all fits together.

We didn't want to involve ourselves in this pool of misinformation and confusion, so when we chose health as our first domestic policy program at the Carter Center, we made our objective the development of accurate information on the gap between what Americans are capable of doing and what we are actually doing about preventive health. We called the program "Closing the Gap." In partnership with the Centers for Disease Control, and under the direction of Dr. Bill Foege (then the director of CDC and later executive director of the Carter Center), panels of experts in the major health fields began to gather statistics and to work on the analyses.

We made it clear to all involved that we didn't want theoretical discussions or fanciful dreams about the future. We wanted concrete information: what could be done with present knowledge by informed people to avoid becoming victims of the most common killers and cripplers.

For a year and a half the specialists worked to answer such questions as: What are the most prevalent causes of disease and death among Americans? How much of this morbidity and mortality can be prevented? What can each of us do to stay healthier and live longer?

We felt like students facing an amazing array of teachers when we gathered for a conference at our center in October 1984 to hear the reports. Much of what we learned was disturbing and some of it shocked us, but there was also a great deal that was encouraging. The heartbreaking part was to realize how much mental and physical suffering there still is, how many American lives are lost prematurely because we do not use widely and wisely what we already know about health.

Our hopes were raised by the seemingly simple knowledge that if we change a few habits we can greatly extend our life span. However, the experts said that changing the behavior of people is the hardest of all missions. A shot to prevent, a pill to cure, something a community can put in or take out of the water, a safety improvement that can be required by law—these are the ways we've made most of our health progress in this century. Efforts to change individual behavior patterns have been far more difficult.

When all the medical and scientific evidence was in, everyone was stunned by the scientists' conclusions: deaths today before the age of sixty-five are considered to be premature, and two-thirds of them are potentially preventable. Moreover, the risk factors associated with these deaths are those over which we have a great deal of control—food, exercise, smoking, drinking. According to medical evidence, a fifty-year-old man or woman today who keeps risk factors low can expect to live eleven years longer than contemporaries who don't follow such approaches. Eleven years!

Having this knowledge is quite a departure from our years growing up in Plains. We could never have imagined then that we would someday have this much control over our lives. A look back to our childhood may help to put into perspective the advances that have been made.

Until seriously damaged by fire in 1936, the sixty-bed hospital in Plains—owned by three doctors, Thad, Sam, and Boman Wise—was famous for pioneering work in anesthesiology, radium treatment, and surgery. A half dozen or more young doctors were usually in training after graduating from medical schools in Atlanta, New Orleans, or Nashville. There was also a comprehensive program for the training of nurses at the hospital, which was a source of pride for the community and of great interest to the bachelors of the neighborhood.

As a young lady, Bessie Lillian Gordy decided to become a registered nurse and moved eighteen miles eastward to Plains from her home in Richland. She and Earl Carter, a World War I veteran and local merchant, fell in love and were married in 1923, shortly after her graduation. The following year their first child was born. In those days babies were usually delivered at home with a midwife or doctor attending. However, the Wise brothers had a policy of making any vacant room in the hospital available to their expectant nurses, and it happened that on October 1, 1924, there was a spare room available in the west wing of the Wise Sanitarium. Thus James Earl Carter, Jr., became the first future president of the United States to be born in a hospital. (Trivial Pursuit games have been won by those having this information!)

JIMMY

During the next few years my father's interests shifted more and more toward farming, and on the eve of the Great Depression he used some of the earnings from his general merchandise store in Plains to buy land. At that time we were living next door to Edgar and Allie Smith, proud parents of their first child, a baby daughter named Eleanor Rosalynn. Not foreseeing that eighteen years in the future our two families would be joined by marriage, my parents decided to leave Plains and move to a recently purchased farm, located about three miles from town in a rural community known as Archery. While Daddy expanded his farming operation and agriculture business, my mother worked as a nurse at the hospital and in private homes and also served as "doctor" to nearby neighbors who had no hope of paying for more advanced treatment.

During those years the standard pay for registered nurses was four dollars for twelve-hour duty or six dollars for twenty hours. But money was almost nonexistent for many families then, so much of Mama's work was done free. Sometimes token payments were made for her services with chickens, eggs, a cured ham, a mess of freshly caught and carefully cleaned fish, or perhaps a possum or two. One of the most valuable payments our family ever received was made by a family whose little girl my mother had nursed for several weeks until the child died of diphtheria. They had brought their daughter to the hospital in Plains from a distant community, and about a month after the funeral the girl's father drove two mules and a high-bodied wagon loaded with turpentine chips more than fifty miles from their home to pay their debt. I remember the wagon being unloaded into the pit in our back yard, where Mama kept her flowers in freezing weather, and those extremely flammable pieces of resin-saturated wood were used to start fires in our kitchen stove and fireplaces for several years. Only someone who has had to get up early every winter morning to build two fires in an ice-cold house can appreciate the value of this gift of instantaneous flame.

Looking back now to those fifty years or so ago, we realize just how concerned parents and neighbors were about our health. It seemed to us that the striking down of children or adults from contagious diseases and deadly infections was rampant, the afflictions, usually unpreventable and often untreatable, coming from mysterious sources. Even the names sounded sinister: pneumonia, influenza, cholera, smallpox, diphtheria, dysentery, typhus and typhoid fever, malaria, ptomaine poisoning, lockjaw, gangrene, colitis, tuberculosis, streptococcal infection, and infantile paralysis. Tuberculosis was the biggest killer of adults, and rheumatic fever of children. Diphtheria was still a serious threat, and a diagnosis of pneumonia, especially "double pneumonia" (in both lungs), was taken as practically a death warrant. All of us were particularly terrified of polio. The visits of President Roosevelt to nearby Warm Springs constantly reminded us that this paralyzing disease could strike anyone, even the mightiest among us. Theaters and swimming pools were often closed in bad polio summers in an effort to prevent the spread of the disease.

A long list of childhood diseases, too, that are now almost unknown or forgotten were prevalent among us. We all expected to have serious bouts of chicken pox, mumps, measles, and whooping cough, and in the days before vaccines and miracle drugs even these milder ailments often led to complications or death.

JIMMY

One of my earliest childhood memories is of a Christmas morning when Santa Claus brought me some books and a Shetland pony, and

I couldn't read or ride because I awoke with a case of measles. Mama forbade me to expose my eyes to any bright light. I remember being caught curled up behind the sofa in the front sitting room with one of my new books. I was not too sick to get a spanking.

When we had whooping cough, our mothers would put all of us children in a room and burn a candle or kerosene lamp under a pan of hot water with camphor and turpentine mixed together in it so that the fumes would fill the air and we could breathe better between the unremitting coughs. Our parents were always glad when we had these diseases and were over them safely, because "sooner or later" they were bound to happen and were considered to be much more dangerous for older children and adults.

The most terrible fear for children was that we might be bitten by an animal with rabies. Our elders told us terrible stories about men who developed hydrophobia after being bitten by an infected animal, and then had to be chained to the bed or some immovable object in order to protect loved ones from their bites.

JIMMY

As a small boy I went into Plains each summer morning to sell boiled peanuts on the city streets, and on occasion the cry of "Mad dog!" would sweep through the town. Almost everyone would go inside and lock the doors until some brave man managed to kill the animal. I remember once when a rabid beast appeared on the street with a long rope trailing behind. Its weird moaning and howling and attempts to bite anything available, including itself, were terrifying indeed. Finally the rope became entangled in some bushes, and the dog could lurch only a few feet in any direction. Our town policeman, Mark Chambliss, moved forward near the dog, unholstered his pistol, and fired six bullets at the snarling animal, missing every time. Finally, one of the experienced hunters came out of Plains Mercantile Company and dispatched the mad dog with a single shot from his rifle.

Among the results of poor sanitation, often cruelly pointed out by classmates, were scabies and lice, conditions most prevalent among children of the very poor families. There was often a struggle among the "cleaner" children to avoid sitting near a classmate who was known to have the "itch," and we were even reluctant to scratch a mosquito bite for fear of being teased by others. But the town dwellers also lived among barnyards and animals, and every now and then one of the girls from a well-off family would find lice in her hair. If home treatments failed, she would be forced to suffer through a short haircut and treatment with a sulfur poultice. No type of hat could conceal her affliction if she had to attend school with her head swathed in cloth bandages, surrounded by a noxious odor.

ROSALYNN

Once a circus came to town for a couple of weeks, and some of the children of the performers came to our school. Jimmy's sister Ruth and I became friends with a girl who was a real acrobat. She could do backbends and turn flips forward and backward and in the air. We played with her on the school grounds, and she taught us some of her stunts. One day we all began to complain of our heads itching, and you can guess what it was. I remember going home with Ruth and Miss Lillian rubbing our heads with a mixture of turpentine and sulfur, and then pulling an old stocking down over it. We had to keep the stocking on all night, but it did get rid of the problem—with a few more days of watching and combing. Needless to say, the circus was off-limits for us children after that!

Health problems drew our community together. We shared the pain and suffering of our neighbors and when someone had one of the really serious illnesses, neighbors and friends would join family members in something like a death watch as the crisis approached. Cars, buggies, and wagons would be parked around the home as everyone prayed that the family would be spared the most dreaded news. On some occasions a fever would break and the tidings would be good. The report would sweep the town: "Mr. Alton passed the crisis!" If the patient recovered from double pneumonia he would henceforth be admired as something of a superman. But the news would often not be good.

JIMMY

I remember Mama nursing my aunt Annie Laurie. We knew at our house that it was very serious, for my mother was gone day and night, coming home only to take a bath and change clothes. When the crisis time came, we waited, praying and hoping, as did the whole community of Plains. And then the verdict: Annie Laurie, the mother of two boys, was dead at age forty-five of a strep-throat infection—something that now with antibiotics would be just a minor problem.

So great was the concern about disease in Plains that as soon as a remedy was identified, the entire community would rally with the utmost dedication to purify our water, eliminate mosquito-breeding places, reduce the rat population, eliminate wild dogs, and inoculate our own animals.

JIMMY

A major event of the year in Plains became "dog inoculation day." All the county's veterinarians, including my uncle Jack Slappey, would set up their booths along the street in front of the stores, and everyone in the area would bring their dogs to have them inoculated. Some came to stay all day on the street and treated the event as something of a holiday. And it was a noisy holiday, with all the yelping and howling and barking of country dogs unaccustomed to leashes or restraining ropes or being near other dogs. I would boil at least three times as many peanuts as usual and sell them all. With this kind of participation from all our people the incidence of rabies, and our fears of it, subsided.

Ordinances were passed requiring indoor bathrooms to replace outdoor privies. Barnyards were forbidden in the city limits, although this was not strictly enforced. When Rosalynn was a child, her family still had a few mules, a cow, and some pigs in a pen behind their house in town.

There was no electricity on our farm until I was fourteen, but a windmill was erected a few years earlier with a tank high enough to provide running water in the house. It was a big day when a flush toilet replaced the outdoor privy, and there was even a rudimentary cold-water shower to supplement the large galvanized tub for bathing.

Whenever a new vaccine became available, every child was required to be immunized before being permitted to attend school. The public-health nurse came to town and we lined up to get our shots. Absolutely no excuses would be accepted because the health of all of us was considered to be at stake.

These kinds of procedures continued in our communities through the years, so that now most of the earlier threats to our health have become rare or no longer exist. Others are easily cured with modern antibiotics.

One final comparison with the past illustrates how much life's horizons have expanded. In this book we are dealing with, among other things, what is called "retirement." Well, in earlier days in Plains, retirement was just not a factor in people's lives. There was no form of social security, and everyone was expected to be active and productively employed until they were incapacitated. Anyone who was "able but unwilling" to work was subject to ridicule or scorn, and those who were truly lazy, who habitually sat around the stove at the filling station or general store talking or playing checkers, felt it necessary several times a day to blame their inactivity on some imagined physical ailment.

Except for nurses and schoolteachers, women labored in homes, yards, or fields, and with advancing age simply chose less strenuous activities. Women of a great-grandmother's generation would sit in a chair by the fireplace in winter or on the porch in warm weather, long skirts down around their ankles, carding wool or cotton, churning milk, or shelling peas. The men who were storekeepers, clerks, mechanics, cobblers, doctors, or lawyers pursued their relatively sedentary careers for a lifetime. Those employed in more arduous jobs on the farms or railroads or in logging and sawmilling usually spent their later active years doing light farm work, or took jobs at stores or filling stations. A long retirement is a modern-day luxury.

With these recollections in mind, let's turn now to today's health problems. Medical science has obviously done its share in eradicating communicable diseases. But we have not been so successful in the United States when our health has been dependent on personal and individual decisions. The statistics for the century show that the causes of premature death today—lung cancer, heart disease, stroke, and injury, for example—are increasingly preventable.

So what can we do with the discovery that our own lifestyle is the greatest barrier today to living to our full potential? The awareness that health is dependent on habits that we control makes us the first generation in history that to a large extent determines its own destiny. We can start by learning the scale of damage caused by modern health risks. That was the purpose of our "Closing the Gap" study and conference. Information is the beginning. And in the rest of this chapter we're going to give you some of that. Many of the facts may seem familiar to you. But try to consider them as new because only by being surprised will we be spurred to do what is necessary for ourselves and others. A crucial component to making the most of the rest of our lives is knowing what endangers it. That has to be followed by the resolve to change cherished customs and comfortable living patterns that are harmful. Sometimes it is easier just to continue in the old ways and hope that the law of averages doesn't catch up with us. But such an approach is never a solution.

Take smoking. Not only is it one of the hardest habits to break but it is probably the most important to conquer. The smokers among us have already heard all the sermons they want to hear about the dangers. Our own children have certainly heard their share from us. We have always felt a little self-righteous about keeping after them so much because we have never smoked, but they have rarely listened anyway.

Now, though, we don't apologize anymore for our proselytizing. The "Closing the Gap" conference left no doubt that stopping just this one habit can actually mean years of extended, healthy life. In his opening remarks at the symposium, Dr. Jesse Steinfeld, a former U.S. surgeon general, said, "Imagine four commercial airplanes with two hundred fifty people aboard each, crashing every day in our country and killing everybody aboard. That's how many people die prematurely from smoking cigarettes every single day in our country—more than one thousand people!" (Compared with 375,000 deaths from smoking-related causes, there were 3,562 deaths directly traceable to cocaine, heroin, and other drugs in 1985.) We would be aghast if a thousand people were killed daily in airplane crashes, and we would certainly do something to stop it. But the consequences of smoking are just as tragic, and yet we've shown relatively little concern. This is some of what we have learned:

Smoking cigarettes is now the number-one cause of premature death and disability in the United States. It is the major cause of diseases that we fear most, heart disease and cancer. Heart disease alone accounts for more than half of all deaths in the United States, with cancer being the second leading cause.

Those who smoke as much as one pack of cigarettes a day are three times more likely to have a heart attack than nonsmokers, and heavier smoking increases the danger.

While smoking causes 90 percent of all lung cancer, it also causes cancer of the larynx, mouth, throat, bladder, pancreas, and of the cervix in women. When foreign substances are repeatedly introduced into the body, the chances of cancer are greatly multiplied, and cigarettes carry dozens of foreign chemicals into the body with every puff.

Smoking not only causes these fatal diseases, but also weakens the body, lowering resistance so much that smokers are sick more often than nonsmokers because they are more susceptible to many other kinds of diseases, and they suffer from more coughs, colds, viruses, flu. Babies are injured by their mothers' smoking during pregnancy and after birth, and the health of nonsmokers is known to be affected by smoke exhaled by others. There is more to the harmful effects of smoking, but by any reasonable standard what we've listed here should be enough. Fortunately, the increase in public awareness seems to be having an effect. The response reminds us of how the Plains community joined together to eliminate health hazards in the past. Among doctors 75 percent of those who smoke have stopped; the figure is 95 percent for specialists in diseases of the lungs. The overall rise in cigarette consumption has dropped, although more for men than for women. And there is no doubt that smoking is becoming less socially acceptable, an important development. Nowadays, when people start to light up they will almost always ask, "Do you mind if I smoke?" This was not true a few years ago. Nor were there restrictions on smoking in restaurants, theaters, and airplanes.

Most smokers we know either have given up the habit or are trying to give it up. Dr. William Pollin, director of the National Institute on Drug Abuse, has said that 90 percent of all smokers have tried to stop. He added that it is "easier to stop using heroin than to give up cigarettes once the addiction to nicotine is acquired." Unfortunately, because the consumption of cigarettes is starting to decline, tobacco companies are shifting the emphasis of their aggressive advertising and sales campaigns to the more poorly educated people of the developing nations. One prediction at our conference was that if this trend continues, by the end of the century the number-one cause of premature death in the entire world will be cigarettes!

JIMMY

> I have never smoked. I have my father to thank for that. He was a hero to me—strong, fair, hardworking, fun-loving, a good athlete, and my buddy when I was a child. I would follow him with pride and pleasure not only on exciting hunting and fishing trips but also to the hot cotton and peanut fields in midsummer. Daddy had smoked two or more packs of cigarettes a day ever since World War I, when

Americans first adopted the habit on a large scale. The government had given out free cigarettes to soldiers and, like a lot of other young men, he started smoking then. On several occasions he had tried, unsuccessfully, to quit. In those days he had no way of knowing that cigarettes would ultimately cause his early death from cancer, but he resented the grip of a habit he could not break. When I was about twelve years old, he asked me not to smoke until I was twenty-one, and I agreed. I kept my promise, and the day I completed the contract I bought a pack of cigarettes and lit one up. I didn't like it, so I gave the others away.

I didn't know until years later that my reaction was typical. Most young people who don't smoke their first cigarette until their twenties never take up the habit.

Unfortunately, my mother, my two sisters, and my brother all followed my father's example and became heavy smokers. All of them have died of cancer.

There is one bright spot in all this damaging evidence about smoking cigarettes: we learned at our health conference that if a person stops smoking, the disease risks immediately begin to decrease, and after five years they approach those of a nonsmoker, which demonstrates the remarkable recuperative powers of the human body.

Other risks involved in heart disease and cancer also respond to individual efforts. We are reminded more and more in today's world of the importance of proper diet and exercise habits, which can often prevent excessive weight and help control cholesterol levels. And a test for high blood pressure, a major risk factor, is within reach of everyone. Like other community organizations all over the country, our local bank in Plains recently sponsored a day of free blood-pressure tests for our citizens. Public health clinics and even drugstores in many places sponsor similar programs.

Another of today's most serious preventable health problems is alcohol abuse. Almost every family is touched by alcoholism and ours is no different. From personal experience we know the effect it can have, and we also know how much personal courage, support from within one's family, and professional counseling is required to overcome this disease.

JIMMY

One of the most highly publicized bouts with alcoholism took place in the presidential campaign summer of 1980, with my brother, Billy, being the subject of a series of sensational stories. My mother always said that Billy is the most intelligent member of the family, and she was probably right. A voracious reader and one of the hardest workers I have ever known, Billy used his natural humor and engaging personality to make friends everywhere. He was my partner in Carter's Warehouse until we moved away from Plains to the White House.

I knew he drank a good bit over the years, but always after working hours or on weekends. He opened the business very early every morning, and was usually there when the rest of us went home in the evening. It was hard to believe that he was an alcoholic, but he knew it even in those early days. Without telling any of us, he even went to a couple of Alcoholics Anonymous meetings. Once or twice his wife, Sybil, talked to me about his drinking, but I believed he could quit if he wanted to. Also, we both knew that to tell Billy to do something almost guaranteed his doing just the opposite. One weekend when he was raising hell, Mama asked me if I could do anything about it, but when I found him he assured me that he was just having some fun with his friends.

SYBIL

It was after we had been married twelve years or so that I realized that Billy was drinking a lot more. He was very strict with the children and often unfair to them. The children went to their rooms a lot of times when their dad came home, just to get out of the way. It was hell, literally hell. We used to have high school basketball games, and in a small town almost everybody goes. Billy would go, and he would be drinking. The children saw him fall down the stairs and were so embarrassed. They would come home and say, "Please don't let Daddy come to the ball games."

When Jimmy was elected president it was unreal. It was as if you went to bed one night and everything was normal and quiet in this little old sleepy Plains, and you woke up the next morning and found yourself in the middle of a world's fair. They expected us to act differently because Jimmy was president of the United States. I think that's one reason Billy started drinking more heavily than he had before—to prove a point, to prove that he had not changed and he would not change. There were times I loved and hated him at the same time. There have been a lot of times I wished he were dead. Lots of times I said it jokingly, but at times it was no joke.

JIMMY

There was a lot of press attention focused on Billy after my successful campaign for president, and his country philosophy and unorthodox expressions made him a favorite of the reporters who hung around Plains. He became close friends with some of them, and after a few drinks would make some of his outrageous statements, relishing the resulting laughter and camaraderie. Later, when he was in trouble, these same resurrected statements, sometimes distorted or out of context, became national headlines. He reacted, perhaps predictably, by drinking more and defying his critics.

The worst victims of his alcoholism were his wife and children, and it also became a serious problem for me. The focal point of several White House news conferences was Billy and his alleged escapades. Sober, he appeared before a full U.S. Senate committee to refute the gamut of irresponsible allegations against him, and only a week before the 1980 Democratic convention I had a special one-hour White House press conference just on the subject of my brother. It was unbelievable that among all the world problems this one demanded so much attention.

SYBIL

Finally, he really got sick, existing just on alcohol, and I thought he was going to die. In the hospital, he decided he would go for treatment, but thought I would leave him if he let the whole world know he was an alcoholic. Well, the whole world already knew. The children and I convinced him how happy and proud we would be, and he went to the naval hospital in Long Beach, California, that specializes in alcoholism. Dr. Joe Pursch, who was in charge, insisted that a lot of the fault was mine, for being Billy's doormat, and that I also needed therapy. Those were the worst three weeks of my life. Dr. Pursch really helped him—and me. For seven years, he hasn't had a drink, and says he doesn't even want one.

Being married to Billy has been interesting for me. I've been angry a lot of times, mad as hell part of the time, sad a lot, and happy a lot. But I have never been bored, and I want to stick around because I want to see what Billy is going to come up with next. I want to be there. Whatever it is, I want to be there. [Billy died a year after Sybil wrote this.]

JIMMY

I never loved Billy more than during these difficult times, and all of us were overjoyed when he agreed to go to Long Beach. I especially was pleased when he and Sybil began working with Alcoholics Anonymous and others who need to understand from an alcoholic—and an alcoholic's wife—that they can also win their struggle as Billy did. It is not easy, but they and many others have proved that it can be done.

Alcohol's most deadly impact is among young people. In the last few years the realization of the scale of the problem is starting to make a difference, as it has with smoking. We learned of a program in Oxford Hills, Maine, begun because of a tragedy, that has saved many lives. In 1979 seven teenagers in that community died at graduation time as a result of drunken-driving accidents. The people of Oxford Hills formed a school-community coalition and created Project Graduation for the next year's class, a chemical-free commencement celebration. By 1984, 129 high schools around the country had joined the project. The results were dramatic. During the 1980 graduation period and in each successive year in communities with the program, there were no deaths, no alcohol- or drug-related injuries, and no arrests for drunk driving.

Not only has the project saved lives, it has also shattered a long-standing myth about health promotion—far from rejecting the involvement of their parents and teachers, the students cooperated in the program and demonstrated their own maturity. This is a program we could all start in our communities.

Injuries kill more Americans under forty than all other causes combined and are an important cause of death among older people. Alcohol abuse is involved not only in most fatal automobile accidents, but also in drownings, homicide, and suicide, especially among the young, and in falls, a significant killer of older adults. And smoking is a primary cause of fatal house fires. What is so tragic is that many of these deaths can be prevented.

The chances of being fatally injured in an automobile accident can be cut in half by the use of seat belts. Cut in half! Statistics prove this fact, and it seems so simple. Unfortunately, the high-risk groups are the ones least likely to use seat belts—teenagers, drinking drivers, and the less educated. It takes shocks like the events in Oxford Hills to make us react and take preventive measures.

In the "Closing the Gap" meeting we also studied suicide, homicide, and aggravated assault, including abuse of children and spouses. The reason for considering intentional violence in the study of unnecessary sickness and death, was, alas, that they are so often closely related.

Most incidents of violence occur within the family; in only one homicide out of five is the victim a stranger. Spouses or lovers are most often the victims, and the risk to pregnant women is especially high. What is most difficult to detect is violence among members of a family—unless it results in death. Wife beating and child abuse are often concealed, with both attacker and victim unwilling or unable to acknowledge what has happened.

There is no question that stronger action to prevent violence in the home could be taken by doctors, social workers, police officers, and others who may know about such abuses. Ninety percent of children murdered in the home have previously been known to be abused, and almost all wives killed by their husbands have previously called the police for help. Arresting a violent husband has proved to be more effective in preventing further abuse than any other action.

We found a macabre portrait of our society today in statistics on injuries: Males are much more likely to die of injuries than females; fifty times more males are killed by police action, twelve times as many from drowning, seven times as many from firearms, six times as many from lightning, five times as many from airplane crashes, and three times as many as occupants in motor vehicle accidents. Among the fifty or so categories of injury, in only two—suicides by poison and drugs and homicides by strangulation (often associated with rape)—do more females die than males.

ROSALYNN

Recently Jimmy and I were running together in the late afternoon and were about a mile from home when a heavy thunderstorm developed ahead of us. Though it was only drizzling and I like to run in the rain, I don't like lightning. I suggested that we get in the car and ride home, but Jimmy, measuring the seconds between the flashes of lightning and the sound of the thunder, insisted that the nearest lightning was at least four miles away. I soon let the male scientist and mathematician finish the run alone, understanding more clearly why men are more injury-prone than women.

We were surprised to learn that 55 percent of all pregnancies in the United States are unplanned. We explored this subject, too, because such pregnancies contribute so much to human suffering and premature death. They lead to abortion, child abuse, wife abuse, depression, a continuing cycle of poverty, and, in many cases, to suicide and homicide. There are, of course, many birth-control measures, but society also has a responsibility to help women make the right choices through improved family-planning services, counseling, and more effective adoption procedures.

Many of these facts appear in newspapers or on television but they do not make much impression on us, especially when the people concerned live in the inner cities or rural poverty areas far from most of us. It's only when statistics take the form of individual human beings that we seem to become aroused.

Our daughter, Amy, had an eye-opening experience when she worked in Chicago during the summer of 1986 for the Chicago Foundation for Women. One of her responsibilities was to inventory the programs in the city for women and children, and she was able to witness firsthand what can happen when someone really cares about young women in the poor neighborhoods of our cities.

ROSALYNN

I visited one of these programs myself, the Lawndale Family Focus Center, which teaches teenage parents how to care for their babies, helps them with their education, finds employment for them, and teaches them how to keep from getting pregnant again. It is hard to believe, but many of these young girls, even after they have a baby, aren't sure what causes pregnancy. I visited a session under way for thirteen- and fourteen-year-olds in the neighborhood that was part of an effort to prevent pregnancies among them, and they were all very proud when they told me, "Not one in our group has got pregnant yet!"

Just as we Americans don't usually think of pregnancy as a problem, we rarely think about the possession of a handgun as being a great danger to ourselves. Our own families have always considered hunting to be part of our lives, and shotguns and rifles are still kept and used regularly. Living in a rural southern community, it seems natural that a good portion of our diet should come from wild game. There are also many people who own handguns for the avowed purpose of self-protection. Yet there is little doubt that they present an imminent danger. FBI statistics show that handguns kept at home will more often kill loved ones than protect them.

A recent newspaper article began with the headline "Across the USA, death came roaring out of gun barrels again last week." The story reported that one woman quarreled with her sister and then killed her with a handgun; a man was arrested for shooting his daughter's boyfriend; another, when he couldn't straighten out his account over the phone, grabbed his pistol and went to the bank and shot the official involved; a man in Louisiana critically wounded his elderly father, thinking he was a prowler; and a thirteen-year-old West Virginia boy found a handgun in a suitcase—it went off and killed him.

In each instance, tragedy happened when firearms were readily available in the home. In a moment of anger or impulse, it is too easy to grab a gun and pull the trigger. And when children find carelessly stored firearms and play with them, they too often become innocent victims.

ROSALYNN

One of the most frightening moments of my life occurred when Jimmy was a state senator in Atlanta and I was at home taking care of the children and running our business. Our oldest son, Jack, was visiting a friend who lived close by. I received a telephone call from the friend's mother, Beth, saying that I should come to their house right away. "Something has happened to Jack," she said. "But don't worry about him. Everything is going to be all right." Though I was nervous about what to expect, I accepted her reassurance that "everything was all right." When I arrived at her house, which was less than five minutes away, Jack was lying on a bed with a bloody towel around his neck. He was laughing and joking as though nothing had happened. What had happened still gives me chills when I think about it. He and his friend, who had been studying together, had found a gun on a closet shelf. Thinking it was empty, the friend had pointed it at Jack and pulled the trigger. It fired. But, said Beth, distraught, "We are so lucky. It only grazed his neck." It had done more than that. When he sat up, we saw the hole where the bullet had come out in the back. It had gone all the way through his neck! I nearly fainted, but managed to get him to the hospital in Americus. The doctor said that our son had missed death by a few millimeters. It could just as easily have been the tragedy that so many parents experience. Just two young boys, having a good time, with an old pistol.

Handguns are used in two-thirds of the cases of personal violence today. And though polls show that a strong majority of Americans want the weapons to be kept out of the hands of at least those known to have committed acts of violence, these efforts have been frustrated by the powerful lobbying of gun dealers and the National Rifle Association. For years the gun lobby has claimed: Guns don't kill people; people kill people. Well, it has been proved time and time again just how easily people can kill people—with guns.

We were surprised to learn from the "Closing the Gap" study that more Americans die through suicide than homicide. The big increase in suicides in recent years has come almost entirely from gun deaths, although drugs are also readily available. The drugs most often used are common painkillers, which reinforces the obvious truth that availability of a method is an important factor in suicide. City dwellers jump out of windows or off the tops of buildings. In the suburbs, where there are a lot of garages, asphyxiation from auto exhaust is common. Reports indicate that many people who don't find an easy way to commit suicide rarely kill themselves, just as those who don't have a gun handy are less likely to kill even in fights and robberies.

Although women are three times more likely than men to attempt suicide, three times as many men as women actually succeed. The most disturbing trend today in suicides is the large increase for young persons fifteen to twenty-four years of age.

For all ages the major causes of suicide are depression, schizophrenia, alcoholism, and homelessness. And although mental illness can lead to suicide, the person who commits suicide is not necessarily mentally ill. The severe emotional disturbance may be only temporary. This is another important reason to keep handguns out of the house.

There is a widespread perception that mentally ill people are dangerous to others. Experts agree that this is rarely the case. Society could defend itself far better if it worried more about alcohol in this regard, since violence resulting in death and serious injury is far more commonly tied to alcohol abuse. Still, when violence occurs, there is too often a tendency to blame it on mental illness. The assumption is that since violence is not the norm, those who commit it must be abnormal and therefore mentally ill.

ROSALYNN

I have worked with problems of the mentally afflicted for years, ever since I first became aware of the needs while campaigning for Jimmy for governor. What I have learned over these years of work and study is that mental illnesses are less understood than almost any other major health problems, and that most people who experience difficulties suffer needlessly. The mystery, stigma, and misconceptions that surround mental illnesses prevent many people in need of psychiatric help from seeking treatment.

Everyone has problems; some people can handle them better than others. A mentally healthy person can cope with life even though it is not always easy and not without some struggle.

Even so, we all need help in times of stress: someone to lay our troubles on or some way of escaping from painful problems, whether it be going to a movie, reading a book, or taking a brief trip. After we lost the election in 1980, I read four books in the first few days. Recreation is always good, and essential for sound mental health; a hobby can be a salvation—something we can throw ourselves into completely and with pleasure, forgetting all about work or the cause of distress. Helping someone else will take our minds off ourselves and can give a great feeling of fulfillment in the process. Prayer also can really help in putting things into perspective. Most often when we get away from problems for a while, whatever they may be, or make a habit of letting go when we seem to be coming unglued, we can begin to see our worries in a clearer light and better decide what to do about them.

As the National Mental Health Association asserts in a policy declaration:

There is a basic philosophy fundamental to good emotional health. That is the philosophy of faith: faith in ourselves; faith in others; faith in the ability of each person to improve and grow; faith in the desire and the capacity of human beings to work out their problems cooperatively; faith in the essential decency of mankind. As the Bible puts it, we are "members of one another."

This is our way of life. It is the philosophy of sound mental health. When it is joined to faith in the great spiritual and moral values, it will carry us through stressful situations that might otherwise shatter us.

But there are always many who need more than good words to help them turn the corner. The tragedy comes when those who suffer do not seek help—often for fear of being labeled "crazy"—or when they do not know they can be helped.

In our "Closing the Gap" study we focused on depression, since it is the most common form of mental disorder. We decided that if we could begin really to understand one of the most widespread of mental disabilities, that would possibly be a first step in overcoming the stigma and getting more people to treatment.

Depression should be easier for people to understand than other mental illnesses because all of us have blue or low times. What separates depression from the "blues" is how long the feelings last and the depth of them. Psychiatrists say that the presence of three or more of the following symptoms for more than a few weeks may indicate a serious depression that needs treatment: insomnia or excessive sleep, chronic fatigue, feelings of low self-esteem or hopelessness, trouble concentrating at work, social withdrawal, loss of interest in pleasurable activities, excessive irritability or anger, constant tearfulness or crying, recurrent thoughts of death or suicide. These symptoms can make life unbearable, but there are many ways of treating them. Deciding to get help is often the hardest part.

Clearly, the single most important message to be communicated to those who need help is to seek treatment. To do so is by no means a sign of weakness. When unhappiness persists, experts say, ask a family doctor or minister or friends for recommendations about where to seek help. Or check the telephone book for a mental health treatment center or clinic, the local Mental Health Association, or an Alliance for the Mentally Ill. These operate information and referral services that can help match problems with the kind of help that's needed and recommend psychiatrists or clinical psychologists.

There continue to be misconceptions about treatment. Many people believe they will end up in some distant state hospital, but the truth is that almost all treatment for such problems as depression takes place in a doctor's or therapist's office. Nor does treatment need to take years; some psychologists say there can be noticeable changes after only a few weeks.

ROSALYNN

And what a difference help can make. Artie Houston, a friend I have come to know through my mental health work, said when she found out that medication would treat her depression, "My self-image improved one thousand percent. I found out I was treatable. I found out I'm not crazy." Her fears were overcome when she understood these facts.

Whatever disturbs and distorts our ability to reason threatens our essential self. To know that the disturbance can be ended, the distortions corrected, is crucial to eliminating the stigma and getting others of the depressed population to treatment and eventually to wellness.

These, then, are the major causes of unnecessary sickness and premature death in our country today that have the greatest potential for being prevented. To summarize, what our "Closing the Gap" study taught us is that our personal habits are as important as the expertise of medical science in giving us a long and healthy life. By following just a few rules, such as the ones below, most of us can put ourselves in control of our life span.

1. Do not smoke.
2. Maintain recommended body weight.
3. Exercise regularly.
4. Minimize consumption of foods high in cholesterol and saturated fats, sugar, and salt.
5. Do not drink excessively, and never drive when drinking.
6. Fasten seat belts.
7. Remove handguns from the home.
8. Have regular medical checkups, including blood-pressure tests.
9. If symptoms of depression or unhappiness persist, seek treatment.

These rules are so simple you may wonder why we bother to repeat them. But we all have a tendency to be like Naaman in the Old Testament, whose story is worth telling.

Naaman was a favorite general of a powerful Syrian king, yet he suffered as a leper. A little girl captive told of a prophet of God in Israel who could perform miraculous cures, so the king sent much silver and gold to the king of Israel, demanding that Naaman be healed. The Israeli king was distressed, assuming that this was a pretext for an armed invasion of his country, but the prophet Elisha saved the day. Refusing any payment, he sent a message that the leprous general should wash seven times in the river Jordan.

Naaman was furious at the simple prescription and went away saying he had expected a dramatic personal ceremony. "Are not the rivers of Syria better than all the waters of Israel? Could I not wash in them and be clean?" he asked in a rage. But his servants said to him, "Had the prophet told you to do some great thing, would you not have done it? How much more then, when he says to you, 'Wash, and be clean'?" "So he went down and dipped himself seven times in the Jordan, and his flesh was restored like the flesh of a little child." (2 Kings 5:1–15)

While changes in our personal habits that can add as many as eleven years to our life span are simple and rarely expensive, and often involve cheaper alternatives than the damaging behavior, they are not necessarily easy to achieve.

As one sensible participant in our study observed, "If you're thirty pounds overweight, could you get up in the morning and do without sugar in your coffee? Or if you haven't exercised for years and would really like to go to an exercise class, would you dare when you would be embarrassed to death for anyone to see you in leotards? It takes wisdom and courage sometimes to take even one of the small corrective steps, but it can be done—even late in life.

"So if you're overwhelmed by the changes you need to make, start on one of these things. Instead of getting into your leotards, start walking. You already have the skill. You don't need any equipment except a good pair of shoes. You don't have to wear skimpy clothes. And it's effective."

Once we realize we can do one of these things, we can go on to another. With each step that we take toward making the changes that can lead to a long and healthy life, the next step is likely to be easier.

Our third grandson, Joshua, was born on May 8, 1984, President Harry Truman's hundredth birthday. At the time of his birth he had a statistical life expectancy of seventy-one years. The life expectancy of his great-grandfather, Earl Carter, when he was born before the turn of the century, was only forty-five years. As we noted at the outset, the average life span of Americans is increasing by seven hours each day, or two days every week!

That is good news, and Joshua will have an even better knowledge about health than we do. He is likely to benefit from a steady increase in life expectancy brought about by the advances of medical science. But he will still have to make choices about his personal habits just as we do. We naturally want our grandchildren to have healthy lives, so it is important to us that Joshua and his parents shape his personal habits while he is still young. It is so much easier than trying to change later.

As a follow-up to our "Closing the Gap" study, and building on the work of many other scientists and physicians, the Carter Center, working with the Centers for Disease Control, launched a new look at "health risk appraisals," which provide confidential information about an individual's health status and likely longevity. It should be helpful and possibly even fun for participants to see just what they can do to extend their life span. To get the appraisal, each person answers a series of carefully selected questions about medical history and lifestyles. An elaborate computer program analyzes the answers by comparing them with the latest scientific and statistical information about the causes of premature sickness and death. The interrelated effect of such factors as obesity, blood pressure, exercise, diet, smoking and drinking, driving habits, family history, and response to personal problems gives a good indication of how many years of life one can expect.

A group of about thirty of us, including staff members and volunteers at the Carter Center, filled out the personal data forms confidentially, identified only with a code number. The assessments were returned to us, along with an explanation of how the system would work for others in the future.

Processing these personal data forms can be done on a central computer at the Centers for Disease Control or within any corporation, university, or local government. Many public health departments and personal physicians can help people with assessments.*

For some time people believed that modern technology would rob us of individuality and reduce us to mere numbers. But that has not happened. Instead, technology and science have given us freedom to act on what we learn, not only about health but in almost every other area.

---

*For further information about Health Risk Appraisals and the results of our "Closing the Gap" conference, readers can send for a pamphlet entitled "Healthier People." Address: Risk Assessment, 5846 Distribution Drive, Memphis, TN 38141.

Through computers, television, rapid transportation, and instantaneous worldwide communication we have a much broader access to knowledge and the arts than our ancestors ever dreamed of. Shakespeare in his entire lifetime probably had an audience smaller than that for one performance of *Hamlet* on PBS. It was not very long ago when even a king could travel no faster than a horse could run; and when we were children, a round trip from Plains of just fifty miles was a much-planned, all-day adventure.

Now, with modern electronics and films, people of modest means can view the paintings or sculpture of the masters, have "front-row seats" at performances of the great dramas, or listen to the most beautiful music of all time reproduced with almost perfect fidelity. Scientific and technological advances have made it possible for us to absorb more information about a wider range of subjects, know more about the world and its people, better understand ourselves, have more time to study and contemplate new ideas, and enhance our individual choices and our freedom.

So our longer lives cannot really be compared with those of previous generations. Each year of life today is equivalent to several years in bygone times in terms of learning, travel, recreation, and services. These vast new opportunities give us, regardless of our age, the chance of a lifetime—our only one—to anticipate the future with enthusiasm.

How We Live

Anybody who can still do at sixty what he was doing at twenty wasn't doing much at twenty.

—Jimmy Townsend

JIMMY

September 1986 was the beginning of my fifth year as a professor at Emory University. Because of last-minute duties at home, I had to leave before daybreak to reach Atlanta early in the morning for my first class. It was a trip of about three hours. We stopped in Thomaston, Georgia, which is halfway, for a breakfast snack and a cup of coffee. Everyone ordered about the same thing, but when my bill came around, it was less than the others'. Deciding that the cashier had made a mistake, I started to point out her error. A grizzled old farmer sitting nearby had apparently overheard our conversation. He looked up and said in a loud voice, "Your bill ain't no mistake. This month they're giving free coffee to senior citizens!"

My face turned red as I sat back down, and a wave of laughter swept through the restaurant and continued as we hustled out to get back on the road. The next morning I ran seven miles instead of my usual four, but even now, on our frequent trips to and from Atlanta, we can expect someone to ask, "Anyone want to stop in Thomaston for a snack? There's free coffee for some of us."

Although I was just reaching sixty when this memorable moment occurred, it was the first time I had been reminded publicly that, at least chronologically, I was a senior citizen. Rosalynn thought it was hilarious and repeated the tale at every opportunity. A short time later, Rosalynn's mother suggested that we join the American Association of Retired People (AARP), which we have always considered an organization for *old* people. Rosalynn laughed and said, "Jimmy can join, but I'm not in that category yet." To which her mother replied, "Oh, yes, you are. You are eligible if you're over fifty."

In the last chapter we looked at facts about health, but the harder job is to apply this information to our own lives. We have been thinking a great deal about how we—or anyone else, for that matter—turn out the way we do. There is no doubt that most of us are products of our childhood, shaped by our home lives and communities. Circumstances can have a profound impact, of course, but how we react to them is largely determined by the degree of confidence we have in ourselves, the level of ambition instilled by those responsible for our early training, the example set by our heroes, the expectations of those we cherish as friends, and the stability or instability of our family life.

Until lately, we had taken our upbringing in Plains pretty much for granted. But it is clear now that the way we grew up in this distinctive little community helped us answer the most important questions in our lives, the ones we are continuously raising in this book. What matters most? How do you achieve it? How can you make the most of what you have?

Growing up in Plains didn't mean we turned out exactly alike. We have spent nearly fifty years of married life learning how to reconcile our differences. Still, we are convinced that the character of our home community and its standards were major factors in determining our own. In today's depersonalized world, it is easy to think of small-town ways as quaint, backward, or idealized by nostalgia. Not true. At their best, they are the foundation for good sense and judgment.

JIMMY

Recently I gave an Honors Day talk to the students at Westside Elementary School in Plains, and then called for questions from the audience. "How did you get elected president?" "What was your hardest decision in the White House?" "How did you feel when the space shuttle blew up with the teacher in it?" "Do the terrorists make you afraid to travel overseas?" Then the last and most challenging one, followed by laughter and applause: "Why did you come back to live in Plains?"

This is a decision we have made several times and have never been able to explain adequately to anyone else. We came home from the U.S. Navy when my father died, stayed here after losing the first gubernatorial race, and came back after we had won and spent four years in the mansion in Atlanta. We returned again to Plains and our twenty-five-year-old home—the only one we've ever owned—when we left the White House.

These decisions would make more sense, perhaps, if our first concern had been to retire to a rocking chair, to a life of rest and quiet in a small and somewhat isolated rural village—which, actually, is what we thought would be the case when we returned in 1981. But each time we have come home we have discovered that being in Plains, among our family and old friends, and in relative seclusion when we needed it, we have been able to recover from the shocks of change or disappointment or, having completed one career, to make our plans for the next one. Plains has always seemed like our proper place, and we have been at peace here.

There are some things that have always stayed the same, even though we have changed in dealing with them. Our basic religious faith and its principles have always been there, for instance, even when we put personal pleasure or financial and political ambitions first for a while.

Having a church home has helped fulfill a need for stability and a sense of belonging for us. When we left Plains to move to the governor's mansion in Atlanta, we went to say good-bye to a friend, a fellow church member, who was dying of cancer. We thought it would please her to hear that we planned to keep our church membership in Plains because we had been members there for so long and didn't want to give up that part of our lives. She said, "My mother always told me that when you move your cook stove, you move your church membership." So the first Sunday we were in Atlanta we joined the Baptist church closest to the governor's mansion. We did the same thing again the first Sunday we were in Washington, and now back home we are members of Maranatha Baptist Church in Plains.

Here in our small congregation of a hundred or so members there is a sense of intimacy that could become too exclusive. That sense, though, is alleviated by the dozens of visitors who come to worship with us each Sunday from many states and foreign countries. We feel our church has a special ministry because some of the people who come for the services are tourists who rarely go to church. Others are very knowledgeable about the Bible and ensure lively discussions in the classes that we teach.

We have a few black members in Maranatha and others regularly visit. We also exchange services with the predominantly black churches in our community—a welcome departure from the strict segregation we knew as children.

Our family roots are deep in this area. In ten minutes, traveling north or south, we can visit the graves of our ancestors, born in the 1700s, who first settled the land after the Indians were moved west to Oklahoma on the Trail of Tears. Our childhood homes are here, and so are the country roads, the fields, woods, and streams that we knew so well in our early years. We know where the wild azaleas are hidden near the remote creek banks, and it is a thrill to find the rare Pinckneya, a most beautiful little tree with bright pink leaves that we understand is native only to our coastal plains region.

We can still talk to some of the same older teachers who, in the first years of school, helped form our study habits and later those of our children. It is a place without hustle and bustle, where we can amble among neighbors who remember our fathers, love our mothers, and who would have been just as friendly to us if we had never done anything other than grow peanuts for a living. Humility for a former governor or president is *de rigueur* in these parts. We take our turns along with everyone else in arranging fresh flowers and cleaning up the church, in activities to preserve the historic sites of our community and beautify our town. We join with friends in visiting the sick and sitting with bereaved families in time of death. There is a feeling that we and our families are supported and strengthened by the community.

Plains is a place of stability, where human relationships change slowly, even while technology has as much impact as anywhere else. We have a good local airport, WATS telephone lines and satellite antennas for television, a nearby college, and a good library. The Atlanta International Airport is only little more than two hours away, and we have a small apartment in the Carter Center to use when we stay in Atlanta. We travel a great deal in this and other countries for business and pleasure, but it is hard to remember a time when we were not glad to get back home. We enjoy just being among our own things—and our own people. Obviously, there are countless other communities that are as good in their own ways. Plains just happens to be ours.

During our school years we were taught at home and in the class-room to strive and compete, and that any limitations on our lives were self-imposed. We memorized the names of artists and their famous paintings, listened to scratchy recordings of symphonies and operas, and were publicly rewarded for reading great books. Successful grad-uates of Plains High School were invited to morning chapel services to be admired and, hopefully, emulated by other students. We studied the lives of great men and women and pondered the reasons for their achievements in life—always including their high ideals, a closeness to God, and hard work. We had spelling bees, debates, elocution, and "ready writing" contests, acted in plays, judged cows and hogs, cut rafters, learned cooking, sewing, and secretarial skills. The best students went on to represent Plains High School in district and state meets, and winners were treated with great respect and admiration by the entire community. Although we were never outstanding in any of these contests, the competitive spirit was made an integral part of our young lives. That was crucial fifty years ago and it is just as valid today.

ROSALYNN

Heavy exercise was an inevitable part of farm life, and Jimmy grew up working in the fields and doing heavy physical labor. We both participated in high school and college sports. Such activities were required of all students when we were in school. In addition, there was always some kind of competition going on, whether it was tennis in the grove—a little park in the center of town—or basketball, handball, marbles, horseshoes, baseball, or other games downtown or on the school grounds. Jimmy hunted, fished, and hiked through the woods with his young playmates and sometimes with his father, and we both used to walk or ride our bicycles to Magnolia Springs, the site of a cold natural spring and swimming pool two miles from town, where all the children from Plains learned to swim.

In these early years of our lives our families were always close. We were together in our homes or on the farms, and shared almost all experiences—work, study, and play. No matter what happened at school or in encounters with other people or events, we knew that our parents, brothers and sisters, grandparents, uncles and aunts, and cousins were nearby. Times were hard in the 1930s and 1940s, and we were taught by example to accept trouble, sorrow, and financial failure with equanimity, basing our acceptance on religious faith and the support of family and friends, while retaining a proper degree of tenacity and stubbornness. In the tight-knit community even the smallest child was carefully made aware of the ravaging consequences of drunkenness, laziness, promiscuity, or other sins committed by some around us. And severe punishment was certain if we were caught violating the rules our parents laid down for us.

Stable homes were taken for granted. In fact, we never heard of a divorce in the community until long after we were adults. Divorce was considered to be a terrible sin that was committed only in faraway places like New York and Hollywood. Marriage vows were assumed to be absolutely binding for life, and any difficulties between husbands and wives were worked out within the extended family. An incompatible couple stayed married, even if they could not live together, arguably a dubious blessing.

The Plains community was startled in those days when a love quadrangle developed between two farm families, and the husbands just stayed in their own homes and simply swapped wives and children. They lived close together, so the fathers and their original offspring had no need to feel lonely and miss each other. And since none of the adults were regular members of a church, there was no need for the church leaders to take official cognizance of the situation. So far as we know, neither the parents nor the children were publicly criticized or in any way ostracized by the community.

With no theater, no recreation center, and no restaurant in town, the schools and churches were the focal points for social activities. Besides the frequent school events and church meetings, our parents regularly scheduled informal weekend affairs, often "pound parties," where each person was supposed to bring a pound of some kind of refreshments. This made it easier for the children whose families had no money. We played group games, danced, and "prommed." Proms were engagements with a partner that usually lasted for about ten minutes. There was always a limit on how many proms could be enjoyed by the same couple, and the sponsors would ensure that wallflowers were not embarrassed by an empty prom card. A stroll through the nearby streets or paths or a more cuddly session on a bench or in an automobile was permissible, but everyone had to report back to the hostess at the end of each period before embarking on the next prom. Anyone who violated this rule was chastised, and the real threat of one's parents being notified always proved to be an adequate restraint, at least for the girls. On special occasions as we reached the age of fifteen or sixteen our parties were expanded to include young people from neighboring towns.

Rosalynn

Jimmy was three years older than I, and that was a lot of difference. When I was thirteen he was sixteen and a senior in high school. And although his sister was my best friend and I often spent the night in their house, I don't think I ever had a conversation with him until he came home on leave and we began dating the summer before his last year at the Naval Academy. Our families knew each other well. Jimmy's father, a farmer and merchant, was a good customer of my father, the town's auto mechanic, and my sister was even named for Jimmy's mother. I was well aware of Jimmy, particularly as we reached college age, but it is likely that he never thought much about me until just before he asked me for our first date.

In retrospect it seems to us that our elders were very shrewd in the way they introduced us to the complexities of the social world. Not only were those carefully planned events attractive alternatives to drag racing and the inevitable sexual testing between boys and girls, but they also prepared us for what naturally followed the more personal dating in later high school years. There was, it has to be said, a strong streak of primness in our values. Marriage was not seriously considered with girls known to "go all the way."

These frequent social events during the Depression years required no cash, minimized the alienation of young people from adults, and let us enjoy being part of school and church. Most important, they gave us a feeling of belonging to a coherent and caring community and guided us to become what we are today.

What we have just described is the life we knew as white children in a segregated society. We worked and played with our black friends on the farms and shared concerns about poverty, disease, and the weather as it affected our crops, but there was no mixing of the races in social life, even—or especially—around churches and schools. In those days this arrangement was never challenged, and it was much later that this millstone of racial discrimination was removed from the necks of both black and white citizens. With these welcome changes, our community is now a much better place.

Within a generation, as we began to raise our own family, relationships between adults and children had been forever changed by the pace of events, by technology, and by everyone's greater mobility. But we tried as much as we could to preserve the notion of shared activities that had been so important in both our family backgrounds. We went camping with our young boys along the East Coast, vacationed on the Atlantic beaches or along Florida lakes, canoed down the nearby creeks, and went picnicking and trekking over the fields in search of Indian arrowheads. We also found time to swim and play softball and tennis, but not because this filled any need for exercise. We got plenty of that on the farm and at the warehouse.

Every day after school and all summer long, the boys would come to the peanut warehouse and work alongside us. They helped by driving the tractors and fertilizer-spreading trucks, recleaning and drying peanuts during harvest season, and tagging and delivering the certified seed that were grown on our farm and processed at our shelling plant. They knew they were an integral part of our family enterprises. And since we all worked together at the warehouse, we did the same thing at home, with everyone pitching in with chores.

JIMMY

> As the boys grew older they developed their own interests and activities, but my involvement in politics gave us another opportunity to work together as a team. Our sons and later their wives participated fully in the campaigns for governor and president. All of us learned about tactics, issues, constituent attitudes, news conferences, speech-making, recruitment of volunteer workers, fund-raising, as well as how to maintain our equilibrium during the roller-coaster rides between euphoria and disappointment. We met almost every weekend to exchange information and ideas and to plan strategy for the next week—and to be with Amy.

Rosalynn

The saddest part about the campaigns was having to leave Amy. We missed much of the second year of her life during the governor's campaign and several more years during the campaign for president. Knowing that she was cared for by our mothers was some comfort, but we longed to be with her and still regret having had to give up that time. After each election, when we were together again, we wanted to take her everywhere with us. The places we went, though, were not the most interesting for a three-year-old. Amy learned to make her own place in an adult world, first with crayons and paper and later with books, as recorded by some famous White House photographs of her reading during an official state banquet. She indulged us by being there, and we learned to put up with the books that let her preserve her private world.

Through politics, we moved into a life we could never have imagined in Plains, with new experiences every day. Naturally shy, by sheer determination we both overcame our fear of meeting the public and making speeches, and were proud of our sons when they were able to do the same thing. We learned not to be intimidated by celebrities, and not to be overly concerned about criticism, as we came to understand what living in a goldfish bowl is really like. And we learned through campaigning all over the country how big and great and diverse America really is.

After the successful elections our children's interest in state and national affairs remained at a high pitch, in spite of being caught up in their own education and profession, and then in their individual families. They were together with us as often as possible at the governor's mansion, the White House, or Camp David. We relied on them to fulfill some semiofficial duties, such as attending the funeral of a foreign dignitary or the inauguration of a newly elected head of state.

When together for meals, wherever we happened to be, our family almost invariably had freewheeling political discussions or arguments on controversial issues of the day. Quite early, Amy learned to join in and hold her own in these discussions, and they were good preparation for the public debates that swirled around us in the political world.

As far as social activities were concerned, our lifestyle changed tremendously in going from Plains to the governor's mansion, and then much less when we went on to the White House. We were constantly entertaining and making guest appearances at all kinds of events. Sometimes it was not easy to bridge two such different worlds—the cozy family-oriented world of rural Georgia and the grandiose life in high office. There is a story about Calvin Coolidge's old hometown friends who visited him at the White House that illustrates the contrast. They watched him pour coffee in his saucer at dinner, and they did the same. They also followed suit when he poured cream in his saucer. Then the president set his saucer down on the floor for the cat. We liked the story because we have been in both situations: we have watched—and we have been watched!

Another important thing we all learned from our increasingly hectic schedules was the importance of settling in and concentrating on whatever was happening at that moment.

ROSALYNN

Jimmy has always been able to change gears almost instantly and work on something for fifteen or thirty minutes when the time becomes unexpectedly available, or as quickly go to sleep on a short plane hop between speeches in the middle of the day. During campaigns, through sheer necessity, we all managed to do the same thing.

I've already mentioned that Jimmy also has an amazing capacity to sleep all night, even in times of incredible pressure. In all our difficult experiences—when the Iranians were outside the White House or wherever we went, screaming "Kill the Shah!", when the Camp David accords were hanging in the balance, or when a crucial vote was pending in the Congress—I have never known him to pace the floor or lie awake at night. I shared his basic view that if we did the best we could each day, there was no point in losing any sleep over what had happened or might happen—that is, until the last year we were in the White House. Then sometimes at night I would lie awake for hours and ponder the day's events, wishing the hostages could come home and that the Democratic party would be united. And Jimmy was right, it didn't do any good!

I think we all eventually learned that being in the eye of the storm is easier than observing it. My mother used to worry about us when she didn't know how we could do all the things we had to do, or when national and international problems swirling around us seemed unsolvable. We, on the other hand, were preoccupied with doing what had to be done to make the problems go away.

There were days, I have to admit, when that sinking feeling wouldn't go away: when problems abroad or with Congress or the press seemed overwhelming. Yet, I never saw Jimmy a single morning when he didn't wake up looking forward to another day's efforts.

The more we worked in the public eye, the more we felt a need for privacy, even solitude. We made time for music, movies, and reading, and we always found a particularly refreshing escape in exercise—and still do. (More on that a bit later.)

We expected to have more than enough solitude on our return to Plains, but once swept up in all our new activities, we still found too little opportunity to enjoy real quiet and to do uninterrupted work, except very early in the morning and after supper at night. That is why we so eagerly accepted the offer to build our log cabin in the north Georgia mountains alongside Turniptown Creek.

The cabin has just one bedroom plus a combined kitchen, dining, and family room downstairs. Upstairs, under a high-pitched gable roof, is a sleeping loft suitable for several beds and a small sitting area overlooking the stream. When we decide to slip away to the mountains, we find a different world. There is almost total isolation when we want it, deep in a valley at the end of a long private road. We have a radio for music and news, but no television. Usually the only sounds come from the waterfalls at our doorstep and the movement of gentle breezes through the dense stand of hemlock, white pine, and many kinds of broad-leaved trees. Wild honeysuckle, dogwood, mountain laurel, and rhododendron brighten the mountain landscape in spring and early summer, and the entire area is a kaleidoscope of colored leaves in the fall.

We were delighted to find that there are a number of native rainbow trout in the stream, so we have been able on many mornings to catch our breakfast long before the sun appears above the eastern mountain. It is easy to find time to explore the surrounding hills and trails, and we have made many new friends among our taciturn but hospitable mountain neighbors. This has proved to be a perfect place to rest, think, and write—a place remarkably free from any outside distractions. We usually take our word processors with us because the different environment has proved to be at least a temporary cure for writer's block.

ROSALYNN

Much as we enjoy the new cabin, both of us have been surprised at how much our house in Plains means to us. It really isn't very fancy, and with all of the children gone, we decided to do some remodeling. We no longer need four bedrooms—one is now my office, and another, which adjoins our bedroom, has become my dressing room. We thought the children might howl because we were changing the house they remembered. But they haven't complained because the remodeling pleases us. And we have room for the spill-over when they are all at home because there is now a small apartment over the garage.

I spent a great deal of time the past year or so redecorating, which was sorely needed. We had been too busy over the years since 1961, when we first moved into our house, to give much thought to it. Now all the objects surrounding us relate to the different periods of our lives and have special meaning for us. On a table in the living room is a small china dish given to us by Emperor Hirohito of Japan. It is not an expensive dish, but I particularly like it because it reminds me of how far our life has taken us. When I was young and in high school, during World War II, I thought Hirohito was the cruelest man in the world next to Hitler. I blamed the whole Pacific conflict on him. Years later when Jimmy was president, we went to Tokyo and called on a sweet little elderly man who raised flowers in his hothouses at the palace, and who gave me the gift. This was Emperor Hirohito—as far removed from my conception of him as he could possibly have been!

Alongside his gift is a pottery pitcher that Amy made in school and a little brass dish given to us by Anwar Sadat's widow, Jehan. There is an Ansel Adams photograph on the wall, and some paintings by Butler Brown and Lamar Dodd, two of our noted Georgia artists. The desk Jimmy uses in his office was an old table, which had belonged to Jimmy's father, that we found in the peanut warehouse years ago. We refinished it, covered the top with leather and fitted the corners with brass. The rug in his office is one we brought back from a trip to China.

Jimmy enjoys his woodworking shop and has made a good many pieces of furniture, including a walnut pencil post bed for our bedroom, which is high off the floor with a canopy that reminds us of other bedrooms in our lives.

Together, and with Amy's help when she was home for school holidays, we put down an old pine floor in her room that we're proud of. And family photographs line the walls of our den and my office.

We love our house. It is home and we enjoy it. And we hope it provides some stability for our children and their children, too—a place they can always come to in times of trouble or in times of happiness and know they are loved.

As we have already said, we are now much more aware of our own health habits, partially as a result of our "Closing the Gap" conference, but also because "at our age" it's high time we paid attention to them. After the "free coffee for senior citizens" incident, our spirits were boosted when we participated in the health-analysis study at the Carter Center. We were pleased when the survey showed both of us to be younger than our chronological ages, primarily because we have never smoked and drink sparingly. We've come to appreciate the wisdom of the old adage about "moderation in all things."

We have usually kept a liquor cabinet at our house for drinks for guests and occasionally for ourselves. Jimmy's mother always looked forward to her one "toddy" late in the afternoon. It was a nice time of day for her and we shared a drink with her sometimes. For several years in the navy, we and other officers and wives from the submarine would have a party almost every weekend, where we drank a good deal. Even after we came home to Plains, Saturday nights were set aside for celebrating the end of a hard week's work. But those riotous times are long past. As our mountain friend says, "It takes about forty-five or fifty years before we realize that we can go to bed at about ten o'clock and not miss anything much."

Eating is another important area where we are thankful for good habits, fostered a very long time ago. Our basic tastes are those we formed as children in Plains, with some significant changes to include recent information. Dr. Thad Wise, senior physician at the old Wise Sanitarium, was a fervent believer in proper diet instead of medication as the best prescription for good health, and he had a strong influence among the nurses and general population of Plains. Although the present knowledge about cholesterol and cancer-causing substances was not available then, our mothers seemed to balance our family diets essentially by instinct.

JIMMY

My cousins and I sold hamburgers, hot dogs, and triple-dip ice cream cones—all for five cents each—on the main street of Plains each Saturday, and for the same price our competitors offered stew and fried-fish sandwiches. I realize now that we were not contributing much to the good health of our customers, but at least there were no fast-food places as a permanent part of everyday life. Dining out, except for community socials, was a rare treat indeed. So far as I know, there was never a thought that any edible food was not good for us, except for our homemade rules that we should never drink milk with fish and shouldn't eat raw batter when Mama was baking cakes.

Our seasonally varied diet came from our own farms and large family gardens. It included a heavy portion of corn products—grits, hominy, and corn bread—plus fresh vegetables, fruits (mostly growing wild), fish from our streams and ponds, and poultry. We consumed prodigious quantities of watermelon, cantaloupe, peaches, tomatoes, and pears when they were in season, since there was often no market for them and it was shameful to let them go to waste (something we were taught never to do). What we ate was certainly not perfect by present-day beliefs. We had our own cows and hogs and ate a lot of red meat, drank several glasses of rich milk every day, and ate many biscuits covered with real butter and sorghum syrup. We boiled our vegetables for long periods of time with fatback and plenty of salt, and ate bacon (side meat) and eggs daily, all with no apparent ill effect. What partly compensated for what we now know was far too much fat and salt was our consumption of the widest possible diversity of vegetables and a lot of buttermilk; our flour and meal came directly from whole grain at the local gristmills, and there were no additives in our food. We now try to retain the best of these habits in our current diet and have changed the less desirable ones. We had to let go of some old delicious habits very reluctantly, but discovered some good new ones. Steamed vegetables, for instance, have a very different—and much improved—taste from those boiled to death.

ROSALYNN

And we've found that sometimes it's not as hard to break a habit as you might expect. I was in the kitchen one day at the White House talking with the staff and I said, "I've been reading that it's not good for you to drink so much coffee. I'm going to have to start drinking decaffeinated before long." Sometime later I decided that I really should make the change, so that evening I told the chef that from now on I wanted to drink decaffeinated coffee instead of regular coffee. He said, "Mrs. Carter, you've been drinking it for three months ever since that day you told us in the kitchen!" We continue to drink decaffeinated coffee, but only at our evening meal.

I had become very conscious of what we ate long before we got to the White House. Amy was not born until I was forty years old and, being more careful about this late pregnancy, I pored over nutrition books to be sure I ate properly. I have been watching our diet closely and counting calories ever since. I struggle with eating habits, particularly when it comes to things like pecan pie and maple nut goodies and eating between meals, and I suppose I comment too often about it. A few years ago Amy told our daughter-in-law, Judy, that she didn't want to be like me when she grew up because I didn't enjoy my food! She is wrong. I do enjoy it—what she doesn't realize is that she came into the world just about the time I had to start watching my weight.

At the governor's mansion we began weighing ourselves every day. We still do, and try to eat according to the fluctuation. We've learned the hard way that it's a lot easier to do a little fine-tuning each day than to wait and try to remove five or ten extra pounds with a crash diet. There are days, however, when it takes a lot of discipline just to step on the scales.

Our daily diet has evolved into one we enjoy and think will keep us healthy. We're still changing and compromising, but we're moving in the right direction. We think breakfast is important, and eat cereals, mostly homemade, that have small amounts of sugar or salt added and are high in fiber. And we have compromised on milk.

ROSALYNN

I liked skim milk, Jimmy liked whole, so we bought milk with 2 percent fat. After drinking 2 percent for a while, though, and realizing how rich even that was, it was not hard to go to all skim milk. We steam most of our vegetables—no more fatback or animal lard and few rich sauces (we make an exception with hollandaise when artichokes are in season). We eat whole wheat or other whole-grain bread and a lot of salad, and I've learned to substitute yogurt for sour cream in the dressings. I search on the grocery shelves for low-calorie, low-salt, and low-cholesterol items, which include some good salad dressings. We eat a lot of chicken, and have quail, fish, and venison from our farms. We've cut down on red meat, and though we're trying to eat fruit for desserts, Jimmy never turns down ice cream. It's probably a good thing that our refrigerator doesn't keep ice cream frozen very well.

When Amy became a vegetarian a few years ago, I had to learn a lot about protein. I bought some vegetarian cookbooks, and have had fun experimenting with recipes previously unknown in the rural South. We eat much more pasta (whole wheat), brown rice instead of white, lentils, and barley. I am no evangelist about nutrition, but I'll admit that I fume when we travel and can't find fruit and a bowl of cereal with skim milk or yogurt for breakfast. I am pleased about the increasing number of salad bars, though, and have discovered that more and more restaurants are serving reduced-calorie meals. We're obviously not the only ones trying to watch our diets.

JIMMY

Rosalynn is an excellent cook, whether she's preparing old-fashioned favorites or trying out new dishes. She has dozens of nutrition and recipe books on her shelves and studies them often. When she prepares a meal, it is certain to be interesting, well balanced, heavily dependent on local vegetables and fruits of the season, high in fiber, low on red meat, fat, cholesterol, and salt, and—most of the time—delicious.

No matter what else we're doing, exercise is still a daily routine. We run or ride bikes together almost every day even when we're traveling, play tennis on occasion, and have been able to do some fishing in most places we visit—Alaska, Canada, Wales, Switzerland, Nepal, Japan, New Zealand, China. Fishing or jogging gives us a chance to recover from long airplane flights and to get away from conference rooms and meetings with dignitaries and learn about people and places that we would otherwise never see.

ROSALYNN

I have to admit that running is not my favorite form of exercise. When I began to run while we were in Washington, it was not for my heart, my health, or to get out of the house. Jimmy likes to quote Jimmy Townsend: "The average woman spends seventy-five percent of her time sitting, as figures clearly show." I'm not sure I'm sitting long enough to be in the 75 percent category, but I have the problem anyway! It was vanity, pure vanity, that made me decide to start jogging.

When I was sick, I got used to exercising to video tapes, and have continued to do that three or four times a week. Still, there are many

days when it takes a real effort to stay with it. Jimmy is just the opposite. He has to have some kind of exercise. He is uncomfortable if he
misses strenuous physical activity for even a day or two, and he's a
good influence on me. I probably would not get half as much exercise
without his prodding. But once I'm out I'm always glad, especially
with jogging. What everyone says is true: When it's over, it feels so
good!

As we have made very clear, for all our travel and political adventures we have not forgotten the importance of the strong family ties we
so fondly remember from our childhood. With Amy in college and our
sons' families living in distant cities, we have had to contrive ways to
keep our family together in the past few years. Our nine grandchildren
are a source of surprise and excitement for us, and we set aside two or
three weeks a year to be with them—both with and without their
parents. Plains is a base for our Christmas and other holiday get-
togethers, and the log cabin in the north Georgia mountains has developed into a special place, which is capable of accommodating all or a
few of us as we have opportunities to visit.

We have, to a large degree, replaced our own parents as the family's
senior citizens who provide a nucleus around which the younger
members can gather to stay in touch. All of our children are willful, independent, and quite different from one another, and these strong forces
tend to reinforce the diversity of our own interests. In wanting to keep
them close to us we make frequent telephone calls, and make a point of
having all of them together at least a week or two each year. One of our
best financial investments is an annual vacation that we have initiated for
all thirteen of us during the Christmas holiday season. One year we went
on a cruise in the Caribbean; once we spent a week in a small fishing
village on the east coast of Mexico; another time we took a skiing vacation in the mountains of New Mexico. Planning these trips turns out to
be almost as much fun as actually going on them. Everyone joins in with
a number of very different proposals about what we should do, with a lot
of friendly arguments and excitement, and then through a kind of democratic process (with the grandchildren being final arbiters) we make our

plans—which we eagerly anticipate for the rest of the year. These annual trips have, so far at least, been successful in preserving by modern means one of the most treasured customs of the past.

ROSALYNN

Although Jimmy and I enjoy being together, at first I was reluctant to join in some things that he liked to do, especially running, skiing, and fly-fishing. But now I'm pleased that I tried them and learned to enjoy them with him. We still go our separate ways on many other activities. Although Jimmy likes to look at hardware, fishing tackle, and books, he is a terrible shopper, and was miserable the rare time or two in his life when he did follow me from one store to another. On the other hand, there are things he likes to do that I don't want to share. He plays softball and goes hunting—without me. He was quite eager for me to take up quail hunting, and I was willing to give it a try. On our first hunt we let the dog out of the truck and she immediately pointed. I walked past the dogs, the covey of birds flushed, I pushed the safety forward on the gun, and it fired twice. I must have squeezed the trigger too hard. I've never hunted again.

We have been with a number of married couples who look adoringly at each other and make such comments as "We've been together for thirty-eight years and never had a cross word." Either they are stretching the truth or they are completely different from us. We've had some heated and extended arguments, but we've always been able to weather them because our basic love affair has not diminished in depth over the years. Interestingly, as we passed our fortieth wedding anniversary, we realized that the arguments have become more infrequent and less intense than in earlier years. Maybe we have exhausted most of the points of disagreement, or at least rounded off the rough edges of those that persist.

JIMMY

There was one aggravation that had persisted during our marriage. Perhaps because of my navy training, punctuality has been almost an obsession. It is difficult for me to wait for someone who is late for an appointment, and even more painful if I cause others to wait. Even during the hurly-burly of political campaigns I rarely deviated from my schedule, and staff members had to go out of their way to ensure that these demands of mine were met. I was difficult on this issue and I know it.

Rosalynn has always been adequately punctual, except as measured by my perhaps unreasonable standards. All too frequently, a deviation of five minutes or less in our departure time would cause a bitter exchange, and we would arrive at church or a friend's house still angry with each other. For thirty-eight years, it had been the most persistent cause of dissension between us.

On August 18, 1984, I went into my study early in the morning to work on a speech and turned on the radio for the news. When I heard what the date was, I realized it was Rosalynn's birthday and I hadn't bought her a present. What could I do that would be special for her without a gift? I hurriedly wrote a note that was long overdue: "Happy Birthday! As proof of my love, I will never again make an unpleasant comment about tardiness." I signed it, and delivered it in an envelope, with a kiss. Now, more than two years later, I am still keeping my promise and it has turned out to be one of the nicest birthday presents in our family's history—for Rosalynn and for me!

In a somewhat modified form we have learned to address similar disagreements more directly instead of letting them fester. If direct conversation results in repetitions of arguments, we have learned the beneficial effects of backing off for a while. A good solution, we have found, is for one of us to describe the problem in writing. It is surprising how ridiculous some of the arguments seem when set down in black and white, and it is much easier to make the small concessions that can end the disagreement.

But what is life if not adjustment—to different times, to our changing circumstances, to shifting health habits as we educate ourselves, and to each other? Jimmy Townsend says it well: "Marriage teaches you loyalty, forbearance, self-restraint, meekness, and a great many other things you wouldn't need if you had stayed single."

Working with Our Hands

When it comes to giving, some folks will stop at nothing.

—Jimmy Townsend

JIMMY

We planned to leave home on the Saturday before Labor Day, 1984, ride all night on the bus, and arrive in New York City Sunday afternoon. Under a program called Habitat for Humanity we were going to help renovate an old, dilapidated building in the Lower East Side and turn it into nineteen apartments for poor families.

On a previous trip to New York I had gone to the building on Sixth Street with a group of young Habitat volunteers. We had to push our way inside through piles of trash and debris and climb laboriously from one floor to another where stairs would one day be built. The place was a haven for drifters, drug dealers, and addicts, some of whom had been building fires on top of the trash for warmth and cooking. Many of the ceiling joists were burned in two, and the floors had collapsed in places. From the top three stories we could look up and see the clouds and the blue sky.

My heart went out to the few young people responsible for the project. They were ambitious and determined, but I learned that they had very few specific plans and no means in sight to achieve the goals they had set for themselves. On the spur of the moment and half in jest I said, "I'll have to come back and do some volunteer carpenter work."

By the time I returned home, Millard Fuller, the president and founder of Habitat, had already heard about my offer, and he called to thank me! He suggested that a few others might be willing to go with me and Rosalynn sometime during the summer. Rosalynn, too? I hadn't volunteered her for the task, and I didn't know whether I really wanted to go or not.

A trip to the big city to work for a week in the sweltering heat of July was not a very attractive proposition. And volunteers, if we could get them, would have to pay for their own transportation and food, carry their own tools, and stay in crowded bunk rooms that had been offered by an old church near the Lincoln Tunnel. There was no information about what our specific tasks would be, and most of the group that we might recruit probably would never have used a saw, mixed mortar, laid a brick, put up a stud, or used a hammer except to hang a picture on the wall.

However, after a few weeks we thought we might have enough prospects to fill a small van—including several professional carpenters, a member of the Americus City Council, a motel owner, a college professor and his new bride—and the list kept growing. It wasn't long before we had enough volunteers to fill a large bus, and we even turned down additional people who wanted to make the trip. Rosalynn's reaction had been: "I don't want to ride a bus all the way to New York!" She seemed to be excited about the trip, though. It would be an adventure of a different type for us, involving no speeches, no letters to write, no major problems to solve, no deep thinking—it would be only manual labor, which might be fun for a change and, she said, a real challenge.

So now the volunteers and I were on our way. The first day of work would be Monday, on which Rosalynn already had a long-standing speaking engagement for the morning. She would have to fly to New York and join us late in the afternoon. The truth is that if she had not had a previous engagement, I think she would have invented one. She felt that strongly about the long bus ride, which was necessary because many of the volunteers couldn't afford to take a week off from work and also spend the money required for airfare.

The trip turned out to be quite an experience. It was a tiring twenty-five-hour journey, with stops only for meals and a Sunday-morning worship service—but it was an exhilarating twenty-five hours. We sang and told stories, and there developed among us a camaraderie that comes from being somewhat set apart from others, joined together in a common and, we were sure, worthwhile cause. Many in the bus had never visited New York or seen any city larger than Atlanta, and the newness, excitement, and uncertainty about what lay ahead gave us a feeling of adventure.

When we arrived at the site on Sunday afternoon, one look at the bare shell of a building—six stories high with no windows, no doors, no roof, and burned and collapsing floors and ceilings—instantly dampened our spirits. It looked much worse and more fragile now with the structure more fully exposed than it had been in April, when it was full of trash. Our hearts sank. And the loudest dissents were from the few professional builders in the group. "It can't be done," they said in chorus. "If this building has been purchased already, we need to tear it down and start from scratch. There is no way it can ever be made livable." To describe their reaction as despair would be an understatement. They were discouraged almost to the point of resentment that anyone—they all looked at me—could have thought of bringing them so far to be part of an absolute fiasco. There was almost total silence as we made the trip to the church where we would be staying.

During supper I invited the most experienced carpenters to sit with me, and asked each of them to describe a possible approach to be followed if we should go on with the job. Soon they were competing with each other to outline the best plan for how our group could be divided into teams, which tasks had to be performed first, what additional materials we would need, and how much might be accomplished while we were in New York. Finally, exhausted from the trip and still mostly discouraged, we all went to bed—for the first time in two days.

Even the narrow and cramped bunk beds didn't prevent our getting a good night's sleep, and early the next morning we piled into the bus again and drove to the old building. Everyone was grim as doubts returned, but no one expressed them. Instead, we all did our best to maintain an atmosphere of confidence. Seven or eight workers were assigned to each floor and the roof, each group under the supervision of someone with experience in construction. Then, donning hard hats, we went to work.

It was dirty, dusty, gritty work, and dangerous for those attempting to rebuild the roof and replace the large structural timbers in the upper floors. Soon we had to put on goggles and masks because of the thick dust that was sifting down from above and billowing up from below, where the remaining debris was being loaded into wheelbarrows and hauled away. It was a long, hard day, but we went back to the church in the late afternoon with a sense of fulfillment, for after only one day with fifty of us there we could begin to see that we could make a difference.

There is great satisfaction in being able to "make a difference" for someone who needs help. The tiredness that comes from any physical activity is all worthwhile, and the spirit sometimes soars. Working with Habitat has been that kind of experience for us. Of all the activities we have undertaken since leaving the White House, it is certainly one of the most inspiring. To help build a home for people who have never lived in a decent place and never dreamed of owning a home of their own can bring both a lot of joy and an emotional response. One has only to have had the experience to know what it means—to the one who is giving time and energy and to the one who is receiving the new home. Soon after we began our work with Habitat, we asked Tom Hall, who had come to the international headquarters for brief volunteer service and had already stayed five years, "Why do you keep on staying?" His answer was, "I see the faces of those who receive the homes." We have seen the faces, too.

Habitat for Humanity is only one of many worthwhile programs in which anyone with a little time and inclination can perform challenging and useful work. There are so many people in trouble, so many needs right around us. We can find programs to help the poor, the elderly, the handicapped, the imprisoned, the mentally ill, alcoholics, and drug addicts, to name a few. So many of our young people need a helping hand, as do our hospitals, our libraries, art museums, and schools.

There is something that every single one of us can do, even the busiest of younger people, but we in the "second half" of our lives often have more time for getting involved. And especially with our life span lengthening and the chances of good health so great, there is an additional stage of life after work when we can devote more of our time to voluntary service. And when we do, as one speaker at a national conference for retirees said, "Everyone benefits. The talents, wisdom and energy of our retirees are badly needed by our communities . . . and retirees who are active and involved have a new sense of self-worth, a source of daily enrichment. The aging process is slowed." That, we think, appeals to all of us!

Helping others can be surprisingly easy, since there is so much that needs to be done. The hard part comes in choosing what to do and getting started, making the first effort at something different. Once the initiative is taken we often find that we can do things we never thought we could.

JIMMY

Even Rosalynn, who often ventures into the unknown, was sure she would only be cleaning up around the work site on our Habitat trip to New York, or carrying tools and light supplies, or maybe even helping with meals for the other volunteers. To her amazement, she was soon doing a multitude of carpenter's jobs, and doing them well!

ROSALYNN

I arrived in New York somewhat anxious about what I would be doing. I went first to the church and everyone was there, having returned from the first full day of work. I was taken to the fourth floor and shown a bottom bunk in a dormitory-type room that I would be sharing with six other women. Though dinner was being served in the basement, many of the women were still upstairs. I soon learned why. There was one bathroom and more than twenty women! Some still had on their dirty work clothes, and their hair was stiff with plaster dust. Listening to them relate the stories of the day and the disbelief at the work conditions, I was even less sure about what I was in for.

Next morning I put on jeans and a Habitat T-shirt and prepared for my first day on the job. When we arrived at the site, I was assigned to the second story. Jimmy was the foreman of this level and had decided that the best thing we could do during the week would be to get down a good solid floor. It was a tall order. Many of the joists had to be replaced or shored up, and most of the floor was gone. To do any work we had to walk on plywood laid across what supporting beams were left.

I was first assigned, along with two other women, to clean up the floor that still remained in one corner of the back section. We scraped up layers of old glue and paint and patches of linoleum that were stuck to it, removed nails that were sticking up, and had made it perfectly smooth, when one of the men came over with a sheet of plywood and said, "Nail it down." Nail it down? Before we left home I had told Jimmy that I would do anything but hammer. I didn't think I could use a hammer and I didn't want to use a hammer. We nailed it down! At first it took me fifteen or twenty strokes for each nail, but before the week was over I could drive one in with only four or five strokes!

The next day Jimmy made me foreman of the back half of the second floor, which would eventually be two apartments. And with three other women and an occasional male volunteer, before the week was over we had laid the subfloor and the floor in our entire section—and with a great feeling of accomplishment. We had learned to leave a nail's width of space between the sheets of plywood we put down so that they could expand without buckling, to measure the spaces accurately, and to use a power saw to cut the plywood to fit the spaces. We were pleased and proud. The last day when we were racing against the clock to get our section finished, we had one piece of flooring left to put in place. It was in an awkward spot that fit around a brick chimney and tapered off at one end. We measured it, sawed the wood, held our breath, and dropped it in place. It was perfect! A perfect fit! We screamed, "We did it! We did it!"

Jimmy came running from the front of the building: "What's the matter? Who's hurt?" When he saw what we had done, even he was impressed—and we all signed our names to that one piece of flooring on the second floor in a new apartment in a New York City slum.

What I learned anew from this experience was something that has been a valuable lesson all of my life. "You can do what you have to do, and sometimes you can do it even better than you think you can." If I can be a carpenter, dear reader, you can be anything you want to be!

Our initial exposure to Habitat for Humanity had not been so positive. During the last few weeks in the White House we had begun paying more attention to the newspapers from home because we were eager to catch up on current events of a local nature. There were a good many articles about our return home. Most of them were friendly. One was decidedly not.

It seemed that there was an organization called Habitat for Humanity with headquarters in Americus, Georgia, our county seat, whose director was irate because we had been invited to some kind of dedication ceremony in Plains that we had not seen fit to attend. The invitation had been one of many hundreds we had received at the White House and had been routinely declined by staff members. However, the Habitat people had taken the negative response as a personal affront and made loud complaints to the regional press. They insisted that the members of the First Family, claiming to be concerned about the poor, were insensitive to the housing needs of those in their own hometown.

In those early months at home, when we were both so occupied with our writing and teaching as well as with the presidential library, we hadn't given much thought to other activities. But almost every weekend, among the visitors to our church were families who had come to Americus to work and train as volunteers with Habitat for Humanity. They were from many states and foreign countries, and all of them were idealistic and dedicated—people who were giving a few months or sometimes even years of their lives to build homes for the poor in need. They were eager to tell us about their experiences, and the more we learned, the more interested we became. When we finally expressed interest in getting additional information about their work and how we might help, we were set upon by Habitat's extraordinary founder and director, Millard Fuller.

Finally, half in self-defense, we asked Millard to come to our home to tell us more about Habitat and to list some of the contributions he thought we might make. He arrived bearing two typewritten pages of suggestions. Alongside each was a place to mark "yes" or "no."

After Millard left we talked together about whether we really wanted to take on a new project. But Millard's enthusiasm had been contagious, and we finally marked the "yes" places to most of his requests. And we've never been sorry. Even for a former president of the United States it isn't easy to find a project that is at the same time exciting, somewhat controversial, inspirational, challenging, unpredictable, worthwhile, successful, and international in scope. But such is Habitat for Humanity.

Millard Fuller was an ambitious young Alabama attorney whose competence and drive made him a millionaire at a very early age. His wealth and reputation were rapidly expanding when his wife, Linda, decided that there was more to life than the accumulation of money. She rarely saw her husband. He worked all the time, leaving home early in the morning and returning late at night. Their two children were growing up hardly knowing their father. Giving up hope of ever being compatible with her husband, she left him and went to New York to be with friends. Millard soon followed, and they were eventually reconciled. They agreed to start all over again, this time with a commitment to let God be the guiding focus in their lives—and they gave away all their money to charity.

Their search for a new life over the next few years led them eventually to Koinonia Farms, a nonprofit farm that uses its income to help the needy, not far from Plains. Koinonia is operated by volunteers from all over the country who come for various lengths of time, work in the fields and in the processing and marketing of the crops—peanuts, pecans, fruitcakes, candies. The profit from these activities is used to help transients and the many needy families in the area. The farm had been founded in the 1940s by Reverend Clarence Jordan as an integrated Christian community in the deep rural South with the purpose of bearing witness in a practical way against a segregated society. It survived the harassment of the fifties and sixties and is still a thriving community ministering to low-income people in our county.

The Fullers stayed at Koinonia for several years, helping to build homes for poor people, and were so impressed with the impact on the lives of those who received the homes that they decided to see if the idea would work in a Third World setting. In 1973 the Fullers moved to Zaire in central Africa. With a contribution of three thousand dollars from Koinonia and the support of many Christian denominations, they launched a program to build 162 houses in the city of Mbandaka. Before long the project had expanded to other villages, and Habitat for Humanity was born.

The purpose of the organization is to supplement much-needed private and public housing for the poor and not to supplant it in any way. No state or federal funds are accepted for the projects, nor is the program based on charity. The prospective owners are required to work hundreds of hours on their own homes and on those for their neighbors. They must also pay the actual costs, which Habitat is able to minimize by careful design, the use of volunteer labor, and locally available building materials. The payments are minimal because the homesteaders are given twenty years to pay, and Habitat follows the Old Testament admonition (Exodus 22:25), "If you lend money to My people, to the poor among you, you are not to act as a creditor to him; you shall not charge him interest."

The monthly principal payments that are required from the homesteaders must be made in a timely fashion, because they are used immediately to buy materials for the next home. This policy tends to be self-policing. On one occasion in Zaire a few families decided that they really did not have to make their payments because they were sure they would not be evicted. All Habitat work in the community was stopped, and soon the village elders were on the radio advertising the names of those whose actions had brought the construction to a halt. Under severe peer pressure, the recalcitrant occupants restarted their payments.

Although prices of houses vary widely from one country to another, the average Habitat home in developing nations costs about a tenth as much as one in the United States. This helps encourage tithing from the projects in our country, with these contributions paying for a home overseas for every one built here.

Habitat volunteers include college students, former Peace Corps workers, retired clergy and business leaders, teachers and professors on sabbatical leave, and a cross section of other Americans with a generous spirit. They work as partners with members of the home-steading families, sawing lumber, making bricks, Spanish tile, and concrete blocks, digging and pouring foundations, erecting stud walls, constructing roof trusses, repairing dilapidated parts of older buildings, and putting the finishing touches on the new houses and apartments. Even small children help with Bible school offerings, while retired people volunteer their skills in every job, from laying blocks to stuffing envelopes.

Habitat is growing rapidly. When the semiannual meeting was adjourned in September 1986 there were projects in 171 U.S. communities and 17 foreign nations, all the way from the low-lying tropical shores of Papua New Guinea to Puno, Peru, a community thirteen thousand feet above sea level overlooking Lake Titicaca.

On one of our trips to Latin America, we visited the Puno site, where the houses were being built on a bluff overlooking the city. The local Habitat committee had been able to acquire the land at practically no cost from the local city officials, probably because there was no water supply on it. The committee decided to go ahead with the project, anyway, having faith that God would provide for their needs. And they found water—a small pure spring, high on the mountainside! Their prayers answered, they went to work to dig a ditch two miles long, through the hard rock of the mountain, from the source to the building site. Not having proper tools, the women, with babies strapped on their backs, got in the ditch and dug with tin cans! They worked from sun-up to sundown, so thankful were they to have water and homes. Tears welled up in the eyes of the volunteer, the wife of a Presbyterian minister from Boston, who told us this story. She said she got in the ditch herself and tried to help. She didn't last until lunch time.

We have had good support from government officials in foreign countries, who recognize the value of new homes for their people and have become interested in our system of construction and financing. A lot of housing can be provided with very limited funds, and, in the process of building, the homesteading families often learn new trades that become valuable assets to themselves and to their community. We have been able to continue the work even in revolutionary political climates.

A Habitat project was started in northwestern Nicaragua in 1985. The inhabitants of the area live in open shelters that have three sides covered with grass. Because of the poor soil and past erosion, subsistence farming is their maximum expectation. However, they have good forests and clay of particularly high quality. Habitat volunteers are teaching the local people how to build good homes—without interference.

When we arrived on a recent visit, the people were hauling huge mahogany logs to the site on two-wheeled oxcarts and cutting boards with a small horizontal band saw that Habitat provides. Two men were making bricks using a small wooden hand-operated press that holds enough clay to make one brick at a time. These are dried in the sun and used for all construction. The same fine clay is pressed over a curved wooden form to make tiles, which are partially dried in the sun and then baked in a homemade kiln fired with lumber scraps. In three days a worker can produce enough of these tiles for the roof of a house. Habitat's only purchases for each home are a few nails, some cement, and used wire for cross-bracing. Because of the high rate of monetary exchange for dollars, good work by the local people, and availability of building materials, we are able to build a home for ten people for less than five hundred dollars each.

Jimmy

Once at the Habitat project in northern Uganda our large dump truck was confiscated by an army commander during a local military uprising. When the skirmish was over, the colonel decided that he needed the truck more than our workers did. After Habitat leaders made several unsuccessful attempts to regain it by appealing to the regional leaders, I contacted the president of Uganda to explain our dilemma, and in a few days the truck was returned. (The commander was transferred to a distant and undesirable post.)

We have enjoyed all our efforts working with Habitat, but to us, the work camps we have led to the Lower East Side in Manhattan and to Chicago have been the most memorable and fulfilling. We have been pleased at what we could accomplish, and have been successful in focusing attention on Habitat and all the good it does, which was our main goal from the beginning. We labor side by side with the homesteaders, and have learned a lot about people we would otherwise never have known. We see at first hand the pride, industry, competence, and generosity of those who in the past existed only as disturbing statistics. They have rarely been able to meet their own needs, but now they are even helping build homes for their neighbors. Some of them develop into excellent carpenters.

After our second summer at the New York site we returned for the dedication ceremonies in October 1985. Jessica Wallace, who had worked alongside us, couldn't wait to announce, "I'm going to be an apprentice in the local carpenters' union! They've already accepted me." She had worked part time in a kitchen until she began to volunteer for Habitat and was chosen by the local committee to have one of the apartments. Now she had learned a new trade—on the job.

ROSALYNN

We ourselves had a lot to learn. One of the first days on the project in New York, Jimmy finished drinking a Coke and took the can in both hands to crush it, when he heard one of our fellow workers cry out, "Don't do that! Mr. President, don't bend the can!" It was too late. The can was already bent, but it was the last one any of us ever crushed. We learned that there are many people whose very bread depends on the money they get from collecting empty bottles and cans on the streets and selling them for five cents each—and the cans have no value if they are bent.

Roosevelt Williams was living in a cardboard lean-to when our work in New York began. For many years he had served as a chef in a Catskills resort hotel, but the hotel had closed and he had fallen on bad times. Now he was forced to earn his living by selling bottles and cans. Even before we arrived he had begun to wander into our building to help with the work. Soon he began to sleep inside to "watch over" it for us. He proved to be so valuable that now he has become the full-time building superintendent, and it was Roosevelt who moved into the first completed apartment.

We became acquainted with many of the homeless people in the neighborhood who are forced to sleep on the sidewalks or in doorways even in the worst of weather, and with others, more fortunate, who have found shelter in dilapidated buildings similar to the one we rebuilt.

JIMMY

One morning in New York I was standing on the roof looking at nearby Wall Street when I noticed an elderly woman just below me in a vacant lot. She was cooking her noon meal over an outdoor fire, burning wood scraps between several large flat stones. I was told that she was called the Russian Princess, and lived in part of the abandoned building next door without heat, electricity, or running water.

I went down to talk to her. She was boiling eggs and corn on the cob, and in answer to my questions, she said she got along fine living as she did, and that some friends down the street gave her water and let her bathe in their apartment whenever she asked. She was wearing an old but obviously costly silk dress and a long strand of pearls. When I complimented her on the outfit, she replied, "I haven't worn this in several years, but someone told me that President Carter was working next door!" She acknowledged my introduction with the aplomb of a true princess.

One final note: My wife has never been more beautiful than when her face was covered with black smut from scraping burned ceiling joists and streaked with sweat from carrying sheets of plywood from the street level up to the floor where we were working, cutting subflooring with a power saw, and nailing it down with just a few hard hammer blows.

"What the poor need is not charity but capital, not caseworkers but co-workers. And what the rich need is a wise, honorable, and enjoyable way of divesting themselves of some of their overabundance." That sums up the philosophy of Habitat. And if you ask Millard Fuller what his goal is, he will tell you, "To rid the world of poverty housing." We're working on it!

Millard Fuller is just one person in our country who has made a difference in the lives of people. Many others are committed to doing good work. And there is plenty to do all around us, wherever we are. What we have to do is look and then leap. So what follows are stories about some of the unsung heroes who have identified a genuine need in their own neighborhoods or communities and conceived new approaches to old problems.

Veronica Maz is one of those remarkable people. As part of the sociology course she taught at Georgetown University, Veronica periodically took her students onto the streets of Washington for a firsthand look at the harsh living conditions endured by some women and children in the nation's capital—once-respectable wives and mothers sleeping in abandoned cars or doorways, with no way to bathe or get water to drink, their small children on streets filled with drug pushers and prostitutes. The problems she saw and explained to students took on more than an academic interest to her. In 1970 she decided to start "doing something" to alleviate the misery. She left the university, and, in a few borrowed rooms, with small donations and help from volunteers, she offered homeless women a clean place to sleep. She called it the House of Ruth, and it is now the oldest shelter for women in the District of Columbia. Maz also found a room in the toughest part of upper 16th Street where the street children could read, play, and get something to eat. Now every afternoon, approximately one hundred children come to Martha's Table.

The city opened more shelters, but provided no food, and a growing army of men and women were rummaging through the garbage cans behind the city's fancy restaurants, competing with rats for the scraps. An old van equipped with huge soup kettles and a serving window became McKenna's Wagon, named for a Roman Catholic priest who had shared Maz's concern but died before the rolling soup kitchen hit the streets. Each evening—through snow and rain and the August heat that drives most of official Washington out of town—McKenna's Wagons set out, manned by volunteers who serve donated sandwiches, soup, juice, and coffee to hundreds of homeless people at various locations in the District. One of the stops is at LaFayette Park, right across the street from the White House, where seventy-five or so people—many with mental problems, some alcoholics, some who have recently lost jobs and found themselves homeless for the first time—are fed.

When Maz tells church and civic groups about the problems, she asks only that people share from their abundance—a sandwich, a pot of soup—but urges them to keep on sharing. Because of Veronica Maz, individuals and groups throughout the area have stopped hurrying by the street people and started to help, volunteering at Martha's kitchens and shelters. She is now working with groups throughout the country to start similar programs.

For Lenore Horowitz, inspiration came in a huge pile of discounted Christmas toys at her local grocery store several years ago. She persuaded the manager to let her have the whole pile for twenty-five dollars on the condition that she would donate them all to the Rockville (Maryland) Christmas Toy Drive. That was the first step in what became project Match Up. Lenore Horowitz, whose husband at the time was Senator Edward Kennedy's chief of staff, had two young children and a part-time job teaching remedial reading at American University, but she was concerned that many children lacked not only the abundance but even the necessities her children had. Because of increasingly restrictive standards, many poor working people had been cut off Medicaid. Free clinics provided some medical care, but could not supply needed prescriptions or even such over-the-counter preparations as iron supplements for anemic mothers.

"There are more people now, more children, going without health care than there were when we came to Washington nine years ago," she said recently. A medical team surveying twenty-five hundred poor children in the District found that eight out of ten had untreated medical or dental problems. The infant mortality rate in the District, already the highest in the nation and higher than that of many Third World nations, actually rose in 1985, and lack of prenatal care was considered an important causative factor.

Lenore Horowitz knew that much of Washington's business is transacted at social gatherings. She scouted parties and receptions for contacts who could provide needed items. Talking to a corporation head here, a public-relations person there, she and partner Elizabeth Wallace (the wife of NBC White House correspondent Chris Wallace) got eighty companies to donate $150,000 worth of prescription drugs, vitamins, food, clothing, toys, and other needed items to clinics, orphanages, and shelters in 1985. They run Match Up out of their own kitchens, have no staff, receive no pay. Donors or recipients take care of the transportation of goods, and everything donated goes directly to the children.

Elizabeth Wallace specializes in what the two women like to call "unserved" food. She got the idea in late 1984 at an art gallery reception. As everybody was leaving, Wallace noticed there were still "mountains" of food. She was told that this part of the lavish spread would be thrown out. She started thinking about all the food that would be left over at the presidential inauguration parties coming up, and began calling around, arranging for unserved food to be donated to the children at Martha's Table. Caterers of some of Washington's fanciest parties now routinely pass leftovers to the 16th Street kitchen. Horowitz asked a McDonald's executive to donate extra food from a party the company was giving for congressional families. He ended up donating one full meal a month for the children at Martha's Table.

Not all the leftover party food in America can solve the root problems of poverty, hunger, and homelessness, and no one—especially those who work directly with the victims of these awful conditions—

would advocate such a crumbs-from-the-table approach. But the message that rides through the streets of Washington when McKenna's Wagon sets out each night is that one person's determination, multiplied thousands of times, can be a potent force.

There are many different ways to meet needs in a community. A New England woman in her forties who had found help for her long-time drinking problem began looking around for something to do with her newly sober life. She had no special skills or training. She lived in a tiny town from which the jobs and most of the young people had long since moved. Most of her neighbors were elderly, as were many of the residents of surrounding towns. The nearest hospital was twelve miles away and there was no public transportation. So Gladys Hagan, of Bristol, Vermont, started a taxi service, answering calls day or night, in all kinds of weather. She saw a need and a way to fill it. She could never afford a new car and often didn't collect enough to pay for gas, but for fourteen years she served her community.

From being a "failure" at forty, Gladys Hagan became one of the town's most beloved citizens. When rising liability insurance rates forced her to end her service, she carefully interviewed all comers until she found a taxi-fleet owner from a nearby town willing to continue the service. She continued to work part time for him as a dispatcher, out of her trailer home, making sure her neighbors still get where they need to go.

There are some local projects that are simpler than starting a taxi service but that can make a significant difference in a community. Late one summer we were fly-fishing during a weekend in the Catskills, and commented on how tidy the roads were around Livingston Manor, New York. Our fishing companion said, "There is a doctor's wife here who has assumed personal responsibility for removing any trash along the main streets and highways. She gets the Girl Scouts and other groups to help her, and now a lot of people have got the spirit, and everyone takes great pains not to litter the town."

Our daughter-in-law, Judy, works for Family Focus, Inc., a not-for-profit agency in Chicago that is concerned about the needs of very young children and their families today. The story of the founding of this organization is a tribute to the concern and determination of one woman, Bernice Weissbourd.

After years of working with children, early in her life as a music teacher and later as a teacher and consultant in Head Start programs in Chicago, Bernice became aware of new research indicating that critical development happens in the first three years of a child's life. This discovery was reinforced by her own experience with children who came to Head Start with limited capacities to learn and, therefore, limited capacities to be helped by preschool education. She decided that something had to be done before a child got to Head Start and that the only logical and effective way to do that was to help parents help their children.

With all her own children grown and away from home, Bernice began a year of planning and working with professionals from the Chicago area and opened the first Family Focus Center in Evanston, Illinois, in an old school building in 1976. Designed to serve fifty families in the course of a year, the center was open for families with children under age three to drop by, talk with child development professionals, participate in workshops for parents or in parent/child activities, or just have a chance to meet and talk with other parents. Three hundred fifty families dropped by during the first nine months the center was open. There were many more parents than Bernice had imagined who were eager for information and assistance, and what Bernice had done was to create a sort of family for young parents and to help provide the nurturing that is so important in giving babies a good start in life.

Today, Family Focus serves more than four thousand families each year through seven different model programs in the Chicago area: three in diverse middle-class communities, two in Hispanic neighborhoods, and two for teenaged parents. Bernice is still president of Family Focus, and also president of the Family Resource Coalition, a network of almost three thousand programs that serve parents and children all over

the United States and Canada in the way she envisioned more than ten
years ago.

Rosalynn

> Sometimes it takes a crisis to change our lives or get us involved with
> a cause. In my work with mental health programs, I have met hundreds
> of volunteers working in mental health centers and in organizations
> that serve as advocates for the mentally ill. A great deal of the time
> those who are involved and really care are those who have a mentally
> afflicted person in their family.
>
> This story is about two such people, Carol and Jim Howe, but the
> same story could be told of many of the thousands of parents, siblings,
> spouses, and other relatives or friends of the mentally ill who have
> come together in the past decade to create a national movement known
> as the Alliance for the Mentally Ill.

Parents of four children, the Howes learned in the early 1970s that
a son, who had enjoyed an unusually successful childhood and adoles-
cence, was stricken with mental illness in his first year of college. Soon
a second son, who had had a troubled childhood, also became ill, and
the family felt helpless, frightened, wounded, drenched in guilt, angry,
and alone in their anguish, which they hid as best they could from
neighbors, employers, and even their own relatives.

Then one day in 1978 Carol met Dr. Agnes Hatfield, a scholar with
a mentally ill family member, who had begun to gather together others
with the same problem at home. The Howes joined in forming a family
group and soon learned that other such groups were spontaneously
forming across the land. Together these groups established the National
Alliance for the Mentally Ill, or NAMI, as it is usually called.

Both Jim and Carol became leaders at the national, state, and local
level, serving in various positions, helping found new groups, and
editing the newsletter—all on a volunteer basis. NAMI transformed their
lives. No longer were they alone. As the organization grew stronger the
Howes began to feel less frightened. Gone was the sense of helpless-

ness. The self-help family group met the Howes' personal needs; it gave them emotional support by reassuring them that they were not alone and that they had not caused the illness of their sons. Scientists, eminent clinicians, and administrators came to their monthly educational meetings and talked about the causes and treatments of mental illnesses, and the Howes learned that mental illnesses are often associated with physical dysfunctions in the brain.

They were distressed by the stigma against mentally ill citizens in the minds of the public—stigma born of ignorance. They came out of the closet and told the story of their sons' illness publicly, and watched and rejoiced as they saw thousands of other families follow their example and take the same step by joining NAMI, with hundreds of them publicly telling their own personal story.

Since then, Jim has terminated his regular job and thrown his energies into NAMI's fight for mental health research, both in government and in the private sector. He now also serves as treasurer of the newly created National Alliance for Research on Schizophrenia and Depression. Including NAMI, the National Mental Health Association, and others, this alliance is well on its way in efforts to ensure that the private sector does its share in searching for the causes and cures of mental illnesses.

In their former life, Carol was a teacher and Jim an economist working on Third World problems. Now the Howes, both in their sixties, take great personal satisfaction in the phenomenal growth of NAMI. When we were in the White House, it was merely an idea. Now it is present in all fifty states, the District of Columbia, Canada, Puerto Rico, and Guam, with more than 625 affiliates and adding three new ones each week. Clearly it is meeting important needs—and it all started because a few grieving people joined together and went to work.

Sybil Carter is another of those people who struggled with a problem in her family, "living through hell," as she said, and now is using her experiences to bring help to others living through the same hell. Since Billy's rehabilitation and the family counseling, she has traveled all over the country, working with businesses and professional groups to set up programs for alcoholics, and participating in various educational programs to teach young people the dangers of alcohol. In addition, she serves as spokesperson for Union Pacific Railroad, giving talks to family members in communities along the railroad line about ways they can help their loved ones overcome alcohol and drug problems. She also helps the employees set up education and prevention committees, which work to eliminate drug and alcohol use on the job.

She says that often after a speech she will have members of the audience approach her and say, "I don't want anybody to know, but I'm an alcoholic." Then she tells them how they can receive help through services offered by the railroad. Recently she helped form a program in her home county to educate parents and concerned citizens about alcoholism.

Sybil could just as easily have removed herself from the limelight and all the embarrassing publicity that became a part of her life, and just be glad that Billy was well and the nightmare was behind them. Instead she has felt compelled to help others, and if possible prevent them from suffering the despair through which she lived. And who has more knowledge, more compassion, more understanding about a problem than one who has lived through it? Her activism has been a rewarding experience for her, and she is changing the lives of many who are caught up in a life-destroying habit.

Sometimes an unpleasant or even catastrophic event can transform one's life and reveal opportunities that could never have been envisioned. On our Habitat for Humanity work detail in Chicago we were joined by Chuck Colson, whom we had personally never met before, but for whom we had little respect because of his statements and actions during the Watergate years, when he was quoted as saying, among other things, that he would "walk over his grandmother" to reelect Richard Nixon. We were also somewhat cynical about his supposed religious "conversion." Now he had volunteered to help our group build new homes for poor families in the community. We quickly saw that he was at ease about his past. Interviewed the first morning on one of the television talk shows, Chuck said, "I don't know what's in store for me this week. The last time I worked for a president, I got three years!" In just a short time our remaining doubts were removed by his enthusiasm and persistence. Even when we were soaked to the skin with perspiration and almost constant rain, he never faltered as a hard-working carpenter, and we had a good time working together.

We were also impressed with the six men who had been temporarily released from the nearby federal penitentiary to join us in the project. We learned that Colson now works almost full time in Prison Ministries and devotes all the earnings from his books and speaking fees to help rehabilitate prisoners as they prepare to return to a free life. Chuck not only labors to expand this program but regularly visits prisons in this and other countries to improve the treatment of inmates and to share his Christian faith with them.

JIMMY

>The challenge of volunteer work is not an exclusive opportunity for people of affluence or those with a lot of spare time. When we left the White House in January 1981, many other members of my administration were also forced to face the problem of unemployment. Some of them returned to their former occupations, and others found interesting work in Washington. A few, however, had worked for us for ten years or more, ever since their college years, and had not planned for a new and permanent career outside the political world.

Hamilton Jordan had come to Plains early in 1966, as a University of Georgia college student, to help in our last-minute gubernatorial campaign. Subsequently he worked in all our campaigns and served in top positions in the governor's office and the White House. Perjured testimony, while we were in Washington, by two criminals led to accusations that Hamilton had used cocaine in a nightclub in New York.

Although the allegations were all eventually proven to be false, the legal costs of defending himself amounted to almost two hundred thousand dollars. Typically, Hamilton refused to let his friends raise money to pay these bills. Instead, he raised the necessary funds by returning to Georgia, teaching university courses for a while, writing a book about the Iranian hostage crisis, and earning additional income by doing political consulting in a few elections in foreign countries.

Hamilton's wife, Dorothy, is a pediatric nurse who works primarily with terminally and chronically ill children, many of whom suffer from cancer. Dorothy and Hamilton became increasingly concerned about these young people and decided to organize a summer camp for them in north Georgia. A couple of moderate means, they embarked on a special mission with just a vision and a lot of faith.

They began by approaching foundations and corporations for contributions, visiting youth camps, consulting with therapists, and evolving a concept of what they wanted to do. After several months of hard and often discouraging work, they had pledges of about ten thousand dollars.

"I knew many of my own young patients who might be interested in attending the camp," Dorothy said, "and we got additional names from doctors at the Egleston Children's Hospital. Then we began our difficult and sensitive job of talking to distressed parents and fearful children, attempting to convince them that spending a couple of weeks with other similarly ill children would be beneficial and enjoyable. We also had to recruit a staff of qualified counselors who would be willing to serve without pay, and thirty-eight children—ages six to sixteen—came the first year to Camp Sunshine. About one-third of them were in the final stages of their illnesses, one-third were in remission, and the others were young patients who had recently been diagnosed and were being given chemotherapy or radiation treatment. The counselors were teachers, nurses, retired people, clergy, college students, cancer survivors, and parents of deceased children.

"The most popular activities were around the lakefront, swimming, canoeing, windsurfing, and water-skiing. We had enough money to rent some horses for the older children, and we also took some of them on raft trips down the white-water rivers nearby. For the more inactive children, we had a good arts and crafts program.

"Our fears of embarrassment and sensitivity among the children were unfounded. Our young campers knew about the seriousness of their illnesses, and were eager to share experiences and encouragement with their new friends. It was really inspirational to see the children in remission talking frankly to those currently being treated about how their hair had been lost and had grown back, how they had overcome nausea and weakness, and how they were now becoming able to lead a relatively normal life. There was an atmosphere of exuberance and vitality around the camp, even among those who we knew were unlikely ever to see another summer."

Every year the camp has expanded, and the budget has reached fifty thousand dollars. The Jordans still have problems raising money, because many foundations have rules against annual funding of the same project. But some local institutions are helping, and the camp seems likely to go on giving children a new lease on life—or at least some wonderful and happy experiences in a shortened life.

In the summer of 1985, at the age of forty-one, Hamilton discovered that he had lymphoma, and he was told that the chances of surviving this particular type of cancer were less than 50 percent. His experiences with the children turned out to be a blessing in more ways than one. He had learned by observing that the ones who got better were often those who did not give in to their illness but were courageous and optimistic and kept fighting to overcome it. With the same courage and combativeness and with the benefit of advanced chemotherapy treatment techniques at the National Cancer Institute, he was later declared to be in remission and apparently cured. Taking time off from a vigorous but unsuccessful campaign for the U.S. Senate in 1986, Ham and Dorothy continued to host more than 150 young people for two wonderful weeks in the north Georgia countryside.

Today, in addition to their annual voluntary work at Camp Sunshine, the couple have assumed leadership roles in a fund-raising effort to build a new wing at the Egleston Children's Hospital.

Country musician Tom T. Hall and his wife, Dixie, have been our friends since Tom T. did concerts for us in the campaign of 1976. (They have been especially close to Billy and Sybil Carter.) Dixie has always loved animals, and on their farm a short distance from Nashville, Tennessee, she has a variety of them, including forty basset hounds that she raises and trains as show dogs.

Strong supporters of the proper care for animals, she and Tom T. struggled for several years with limited success to finance the local humane society. Finally, Dixie, a native of England, decided to put some of the Southern native crops and recipes to good use. She began collecting fruits and vegetables during the season and, on an increasing scale, transforming them into delicious relishes, pickles, chowchows, jellies, jams, preserves, and sauces.

Aside from collecting all the produce she can from friends in her home area, each year in early summer she drives to Plains and, with the help of Sybil Carter and a few other women, spends a week in the hot sun harvesting the enormous crops of wild plums and blackberries alongside the roads and trails on our farms. She carries the fruit back home to Nashville, where she and other volunteers do the canning and preserving. She and Tom T. market the attractively labeled jars during the remainder of the year and have raised several hundred thousand dollars.

The Halls are now building a center for the care, training, and enjoyment of animals. Called Animal Land, it will house homeless animals, train dogs as companions for the blind, offer instructions to owners in the proper care of their pets, and be a place where children can become familiar with different kinds of creatures.

Even before the project is finished, Dixie has begun to bring handicapped children to the "farm" to ride horses. She said watching these children, most of whom have never seen a real horse, have the thrill of touching and actually getting on one has been worth all the effort that has gone into making Animal Land a reality. Beginning as a hobby, this project has now become almost a full-time effort for Dixie and some of her friends, who do all the work themselves.

One of the earliest settlers in the tiny southwest Georgia town of Lumpkin, twenty-five miles from Plains, was a German immigrant shoe-maker named Singer. More than a century later the Singers were still a leading family in the community, but they sadly watched as their community became more and more rundown. The town's future looked as bleak as the long-empty stagecoach inn on the courthouse square, which was in desperate need of restoration and a coat of paint.

Fortunately for Lumpkin, there was Joe Mahan, a director at the historical museum in Columbus, Georgia, who was an expert on Georgia Indians and the early history of our state. Joe had heard of a collection of old houses, tools, and machinery for which the owners were seeking a home at about the same time the people in Lumpkin were looking for something to revive their town.

Joe knew how the Rockefeller-sponsored restoration at Williamsburg had made it possible for people from all over the world to experience what the colonial Virginia capital had been like when George Washington, Thomas Jefferson, and Patrick Henry walked its streets. His ambitions were more modest—the reconstruction of an authentic rural village of the 1850s. Lumpkin is near Columbus and was a natural choice, so he approached the community leaders with his idea. Ann Singer and others responded enthusiastically, and she was chosen chairman of the hometown group.

Substituting hard work and community spirit for large sums of money, they went to work. They restored the old stagecoach stop at the center of town to its original simple beauty, and the whole community began to fix itself up. There were a fair number of antebellum houses scattered around Lumpkin, but they couldn't very well get everyone to move them all to one place for a "town." So Ann and a small group of interested townfolk got their first buildings from the collection that Joe

Mahan had discovered. And as others heard about what they were doing, people from nearby communities contributed abandoned one-room office buildings and farm structures, often complete with the old law or medical books, implements, and hand tools of their early owners. Houses were offered, including late Federal, Greek Revival, and early Victorian styles. Anytime an old building was doomed for destruction or people feared it would decay and be lost where it was, they offered it to the village. Each one had to be carefully taken apart, with the boards numbered, and put back together with painstaking precision on a hilly, tree-shaded field near Lumpkin. Joe Mahan helped document details. Soon they had churches, a school, a courthouse, blacksmith and pottery and gun shops, a mule-operated cotton gin, and a variety of small and large houses. Not all were from Ann's county, but each was an authentic building of the period, often almost unchanged since its creation.

The town of Westville did not exist in 1850, but unlike Disneyland and other made-up frontier villages, everything in Westville was used in Georgia around 1850 for the purpose for which it is now used. The hand-planed boards and family-made pieces of furniture, like the biscuits cooked in a big Dutch oven in a huge fireplace in one of the oldest houses, are real. Blacksmiths make nails and hooks and implements, mules turn the cotton gin, the pews are back in the churches, the books in the school, candles on the sideboards, and fire in the forge. Very few planes fly over, so even the sounds can be authentic. Westville is still growing as new additions are offered, and it has given Lumpkin a new lease on life.

The problems, methods, and resources differ, but all of these people have found practical ways to help with real problems. Some have seen a need and worked to fulfill it; some use their life experiences to help those who share similar problems, while others use their own special talents to help the less fortunate, either out of a religious commitment or just to share their blessings.

Though the motivations have been different, the end results have been better lives for many who have been directly affected. These stories inspire us to want to do something, to take action, to look around and learn about our own community needs. And the rewards come for all, not only for those who are helped. People who reach out to others are rarely lonely or bored.

At a Plains Lions Club Christmas party we had a competitive quiz about our own community, and two of the questions were: (a) "How many widows are there in Plains?" and (b) "How many widowers?" The answers were (a) 32, and (b) 1. We all sat around and talked for a few minutes about the lonely women who lived among us, and then we began to realize that most of them managed to stay quite busy with regular jobs and others were invaluable in carrying out the many volunteer projects that made our town a pleasant place to live.

One doesn't necessarily have to start something new to become involved in an interesting project. In many communities, clearinghouses help match the talents and interests of volunteers to the needs. Also, it is easy to find out about groups not listed in the telephone book through social-service agencies or newspapers. Sometimes a telephone call is all it takes, with the question "What can I do to help?"

The answer is as varied as America's communities and their needs and resources, as different as our individual talents and ideas and dreams. There is no one thing that would be best for everyone.

Volunteers work with families of jailed inmates, help find homes for stray animals, translate school notices for parents who cannot read English, prepare and serve meals-on-wheels to housebound elderly and disabled people. Specially trained volunteers describe the crucial action onstage to blind playgoers. Others read tests or research materials to disabled students, help with poetry writing or drama groups at retirement homes, work with teenaged mothers at day-care centers that allow them to continue their schooling and help them with nutrition, budgeting, and parenting skills.

Volunteers have had a major impact on the environment, pointing out problems long before officials or even scientists recognized them, and saving endangered species and irreplaceable natural areas. Tourists, "driftwood" collectors, and others, even cross-burning Ku Klux Klan mobs in days gone by, trampled and destroyed much of the very special vegetation that grows in small patches of dirt and even out of the bare rock of Georgia's Stone Mountain, the largest exposed piece of granite in the world. But a group of concerned citizens managed to acquire and preserve (when Jimmy was governor) the only other similar spot—Stone Mountain's smaller twin Panola Mountain—with the help of the Nature Conservancy, until it could be made a state-owned preserve and research area. Similar efforts by individuals saved several of Georgia's lovely sea islands, including the largest, Cumberland, now a national seashore.

Special Olympics groups need many "huggers" to encourage retarded athletes, and some hospital nurseries use volunteer huggers to stimulate low-birth-weight babies before they are strong enough to go home. Hospital emergency rooms can be frightening places, and some hospitals use volunteers in emergency rooms to help sick and injured people and their families in nonmedical ways.

JIMMY

We decided it would be a good idea to look around one afternoon to see what is available in our immediate area for anyone who is interested in getting involved in community affairs or working as a volunteer, or just in doing something different for enjoyment. Rosalynn volunteered to make a tour of our local college, library, hospital, and mental health center, and we were surprised at the opportunities right here in our own backyard.

ROSALYNN

I went first to Georgia Southwestern College, where we were both students, and talked with the head of the department of continuing education, Bobbie Duncan. There were some very interesting subjects offered—some that I would like to take when I have the time. For instance, a course in the art of stained glass, in which students actually make a window panel; a course in memory power that "will uncover your natural ability to memorize facts, figures and events" (I need that!); a glass-blowing class; a basic cardiac life-support course to train the average person to perform cardiopulmonary resuscitation (CPR); a self-defense course in which one "learns how to avoid being a victim . . . designed for all age groups, men, women and children." There were also swim classes, exercise classes, workshops on oil painting, investment strategies for the 1980s, public speaking, writing, and computer operation. All of these were in addition to the regular curriculum and courses in updating business skills.

Although the classes at the college are not designed specifically for the retired, they do attract many older people. There are some who like to do "different" things and many who are just at home and bored and looking for an interesting pastime. The college also offers a place to others who want to exercise but don't like to do it alone, or who come on doctor's orders for a daily swim.

One of the most interesting offerings of the college for those our age is a program called Elderhostel. One of the reasons we had thought about going to the college in the first place was that we wanted to find out about this particular program. Several times each year we have groups of visitors come to our church who are participating in it, and from their description it seemed like a very good way to have an exciting time and learn something in the process.

> Elderhostel is an educational program for older adults who want to expand their horizons and develop new interests and enthusiasms . . . our commitment is to the belief that retirement does not represent an end to significant activity . . . but a new beginning filled with opportunities and challenges.
>
> With Elderhostel, participants enjoy inexpensive, short-term academic programs at educational institutions around the world. . . . They live on campus, eat in the cafeteria, and have access to the cultural and recreational facilities and resources available there.

Thus begins the explanation in the Elderhostel catalog, which is sent to every public library and branch facility in the United States and

Canada. The program is patterned after the youth hostels of Europe and the folk schools of Scandinavia, but is designed for citizens over sixty (and spouses). Almost everyone can find a program close by because they are offered in over 850 colleges, universities, and other educational institutions—in all fifty states, all provinces of Canada, and over twenty countries overseas. Or better still, one can come to Georgia in late spring or early autumn! There are programs in twenty-three colleges, one of our most popular being near the beaches of our beautiful Georgia coast.

The college director said that the Elderhostel program had become her favorite. "We meet so many interesting people from all over the country who just want to stay abreast of new things. We've enrolled hostelers who have Ph.D.'s and others who have never graduated from high school. They are wonderful, and they are not 'old.' We've had people in wheelchairs, while others you see early in the morning jogging around the exercise trails on the campus. One couple wrote that they would like to play tennis and would need partners—not just any partners, but good ones. We paired them with our tennis pros, and they gave them a run for their money.

"For our winter session we offered courses in Georgia history in a Southern setting featuring the Civil War prison at nearby Andersonville; Victorian architecture; and Plains, hometown of a president; seismology, reviewing the occurrence and distribution of earthquakes (right after the disaster in Mexico); and exploring poetry, from Shakespeare's sonnets to the works of Dylan Thomas. When Halley's comet was approaching we had a session on astronomy, featuring the comet. We just have fun."

Most programs are one week in length. The courses are not for credit and there are no exams, grades, or required homework. And no particular previous knowledge or study is required. The cost of the program at Georgia Southwestern is $190, which includes room and board, and many of those who come here go on to another college in Georgia for an additional week.

There is another advantage of the Elderhostel program or in returning to school of older students for further study. It serves to break down the barrier of age segregation, and the mix of all ages is of benefit to everyone, young or old. The young can learn from the experience of mature adults, while the returning student can stay in touch with the customs of today's youth, however incomprehensible they may sometimes be to those of us who grew up in simpler and more naive times.

ROSALYNN

From the college I went to our local public library, and one of the first things I saw was an Elderhostel catalog! I asked the librarian if they had any specific programs for older people. She said, "We have large-print books and books on tape." How we are stereotyped! When I explained that that was not what I had in mind, although it was good to know the library had such things, she said they had no special programs for adults but many for children. So I asked if they could use volunteers. "Oh, yes" was the reply. "We're always short of help and never have enough volunteers. We need people for shelving [which I learned was putting books back on the shelves], especially in the summer when children check out three times the normal number of books. We're computerizing the library, and need typists who can put the names and authors of books on the computer, and we need help with research. We also have a hundred years of the *Times-Recorder* [our local daily newspaper] that need indexing, and we'll probably never get it done unless volunteers do it." Wouldn't it be fun to look at the newspapers of a hundred years ago!

I went next to the local hospital where Jimmy had served on the Hospital Authority and I had been a member of the auxiliary. In the lobby I met a Pink Lady, who had been working during the afternoon and was on her way home. She told me that she had been volunteering for thirteen years, ever since she moved to our community from Indiana and had become homesick. The work had given her a great feeling of satisfaction because it helped the nurses and patients so much, and she had quickly met and made lifelong friends. In order to qualify as a Pink Lady, she paid dues of two dollars per year to be a member of the auxiliary and gave fifty hours of service to the hospital. She told me of one elderly person in the community who got a special award every year for eight hundred hours of work.

Almost every hospital has an auxiliary whose members perform necessary functions. The purpose of the organization is twofold: to raise money for projects and to provide volunteers. At our hospital the members manage and run the gift shop and also make and donate gift items for sale. They have bake sales and approach individuals and civic organizations for donations. In the past two years they have raised over twenty-five thousand dollars to pay for part of the remodeled maternity section. They were working this summer to buy a new monitor for the recovery room.

The Pink Ladies like to say they "add a little cheer, and let the nurses take care of the patients." They act as receptionists, serve coffee to people in the waiting rooms; deliver mail, flowers, and gifts; water plants; and run errands for patients and employees at desks. In some hospitals they are allowed to carry medical records and to bring prescriptions to the pharmacy. They cannot give any food or medicine to a patient. "We can water the flowers but we can't water the patients!" On special occasions, such as Valentine's Day, Halloween, Thanksgiving, and Christmas, they make tray favors. They help with the Bloodmobile and with health fairs. Trained persons help with secretarial work. "We try to be flexible and do whatever the administrator asks us to do," a Pink Lady said.

These women have a few other reasons for liking the work: "We have a wonderful time and make great friends," and "The color pink is so flattering. Someone's bound to tell you that you look good!"

ROSALYNN

I have worked with many good and worthwhile causes when we searched for people to become involved. Almost every mental health center has a volunteer program, where those willing are trained to feed helpless children, read stories to them, plant flower beds with geriatric patients, or just visit and be a friend to someone in trouble. So often, the best therapy for a mentally ill person is just knowing that someone cares.

When I arrived at our local mental health center, even though it was the end of a long day, everything was still bustling. One of the staff persons, a psychiatric nurse, told me that she had served as a volunteer before she began working full time, and her job had been to take "members" shopping and to the library to check out books or to watch movies and other films. Our local center is no different from others around the country. Funds are short and so many services are needed. I was given a long memorandum listing the activities for volunteers. Everyone can find something on the list to do. It included leading members in musical activities, outdoor sports, arts and crafts programs, exercise programs, socials (usually at night or on weekends), flower gardening activities, and publishing a newsletter.

Many churches and synagogues have effective outreach programs. Members of our little church in Plains make a modest effort to respond to the needs of our community. We contribute clothes to the local clothing bank for the needy, and minister to elderly citizens in our convalescent home. When the house of an elderly man burned down recently, we bought clothes for him and helped him furnish another place to live. We contribute to a transient fund that provides meals, food, gas, and sometimes overnight stays at a local motel or a bus ticket for stranded travelers who come through our town. And we visit shut-ins and the sick.

Some congregations do much more. The best example we have seen lately of a church serving the community is Bethel Lutheran Church in Chicago that hosted our most recent Habitat work group. If that small congregation in one of the poorest neighborhoods in Chicago can operate three programs for senior citizens, a twelve-hour, twelve-month day-care program for children, and provide meals-on-wheels, employment and housing services for its members, what might more affluent churches be able to do in their communities?

We were impressed with board member Annie Liddell's description of how members with jobs who could not afford to give more would lend money they would need later to the church and let the church finance some of its projects on the interest. In a time when social programs are being cut back, that kind of creative financing helps to get around some of the seemingly intractable barriers to giving poor people a chance.

Some affluent churches are setting good examples. A large Presbyterian church in Alexandria, Virginia, has adopted a town in Appalachian Kentucky, with young and old going down on work projects several times a year, helping eliminate malnutrition among children and establishing a long-term relationship of friendship and respect. One of the volunteers with us in Chicago, Ed Smith, pastor of a Lutheran church in Colorado, was taking a group of his young people to an Indian reservation the next week for a work project, something they do regularly. Our church in Atlanta set up a clinic for testing eyes and ears of children in a poverty section of town.

It is obvious that voluntary public service can take many forms and that the opportunities are there if we just take advantage of them. For us it has brought new interests, better understanding of old problems, and a whole new circle of friends. And even though every community does not have a Habitat for Humanity (they're easy to start!), and few people can set up a Camp Sunshine for terminally ill children, preserve a community of the 1850s, or work with Tom T. and Dixie Hall in establishing an animal shelter, there is still a constant need for volunteers in every community and hundreds of ways one can be of help to others.

ROSALYNN

When my mother was forced to retire from the post office at age seventy, she was devastated. It happened during our presidential campaign, and I was off on a trip. When I returned home for the weekend, my brother said to me, "Mother has been crying all week." This was unusual. I went to her and said that I thought she would enjoy not having to get up and be at work every morning at seven o'clock. She said, "It's not that. It's just that nobody thinks I can do good work anymore."

Within a week we had asked her to be a volunteer. She went to Florida to baby-sit with our grandson Jason, so that Jack and Judy, who had moved to Florida to campaign, could both be free to get out and work at the same time. From then on she had plenty to do, and she knew that she was needed. After the campaign, while we were in Washington, she began to work a few hours each day for our local florist, carrying flowers and plants to the sick and shut-ins in the community. She began to take trips occasionally with friends, some of whom she had not known until she became involved in the campaign. In her eighties, she remains active, working, traveling, being a good mother, grandmother, and great-grandmother, doing volunteer work for several hours each week in the Plains welcome center, meeting new people who involve her in new experiences—enjoying the second part of her life.

One more thought: Pick out a good candidate for public office and volunteer to help in the campaign. There is always a need, and you will be appreciated more than you will ever know. We can vouch for that from personal experience. And, who knows, you may be able to make a great difference in the way our government works. We needed a lot more volunteers in 1980!

Away from Home

Most evenings, like millions of other Americans, we sit in front of our television sets and watch the daily news. We grieve with the starving Ethiopians; we witness the bombings and destruction of human lives in Lebanon, the mounting tensions and death toll in South Africa; we see the plight of refugees fleeing for their lives from many lands, with nowhere left to call home; we are told of the oppression of people who do not have the freedom to worship, to assemble peacefully or express their views publicly, many of whom are imprisoned without cause, or even murdered by their own government. Traveling around the country we see homeless men and women sleeping on steam grates, in open doorways or under newspapers on the city sidewalks of the richest nation on earth. There is no way to become inured to the misery that abounds. We, like everyone else, are more aware of the world around us than ever before in history.

It was different when we were children growing up in Plains. In those days, during the Depression, we lived sheltered and isolated lives. In hard times and with few modern conveniences, people struggled just to provide for their own families. With no television, few radios and newspapers, and rare opportunities to travel even to neighboring towns, the outside world seemed very remote. It was not until the young men of our town were called away to serve the country in World War II that the boundaries of our world began to expand. We got our news then from the relatively impersonal newspapers and radios. The intimate images of the television screen were not yet a part of our lives.

Even after we were married and had come back home from the navy in the 1950s, Plains was still not too concerned with national and international affairs. There were some things that directly affected our daily lives, especially the civil rights question, but political matters for us did not usually extend to other national issues. Most well-informed people could probably have named our U.S. senators, which was not hard since southern senators changed only once every generation or two in those days. One of them, Senator Herman Talmadge, had even been to speak at Plains High School once and had dinner in the Carter home—quite an exciting event for our town. But with the exception of the president and possibly the secretary of agriculture (a very considerable figure thereabouts, whichever party was in power), few people could have named any other leaders in Washington.

Having been away in the navy, traveled widely, and developed a lively interest in politics, we became the "authorities" on Main Street about national affairs—at least to our families and friends.

ROSALYNN

One day when I was sitting at my desk in the warehouse office, my mother, who worked in the post office, came in to tell us that a large billboard had been erected close to town which read, "Impeach Earl Warren," and nobody around the post office knew who he was. I explained to her that Earl Warren was Chief Justice of the Supreme Court, at that time much in the news and under fire by conservatives for his "liberal" court decisions on school desegregation. John Birch signs were springing up in protest all over the South.

The time of unawareness of national and international events for the people of Plains has changed, for more reasons than one! But with the advent of television the world has become smaller for all of us everywhere. The major current events and disastrous happenings become part of our lives as we live with them day by day through the images on our television screens. It is inevitable that we become concerned and maybe even feel some responsibility for them.

For those of us who wish to be involved—or stay involved, as the case may be—there are many opportunities, not only to become more informed about the issues that interest us most, but also to participate actively in solutions to the problems that present themselves. In recent years the avenues opened for broader study, travel, and service have multiplied. In our own work and travels, we have come in contact with many who have found ways to expand their horizons and to participate in areas beyond the boundaries of their own communities. Some of these are rich and famous, while others are ordinary citizens, but all have the same desire: to make their lives meaningful and significant in service to others.

But how is it possible to expand our interests and activities beyond our own home community? It is not easy to know how to invest time, talents, or money in learning and helping, even when we have a natural interest in a subject or problem. However, there are literally scores of organizations and programs designed to match concerned Americans with rewarding activities, and there can also be extra satisfaction in creating our own opportunities. After we left the White House this was another of our major challenges. We wanted not only to build on old interests but to create some new projects that would take advantage of our special opportunities.

We have found the forum for these objectives through the work of the Carter Presidential Center. From the germ of an idea born in the middle of the night to its full conception, through the planning stages, fund-raising, construction, and finally its formal opening in October 1986, we have watched the center become a reality. It has been demanding, time-consuming, frustrating, gratifying.

Obviously, the establishment of a presidential center is not something we can urge readers to try for themselves. But because we believe the work there is a valuable resource for the country—and getting the center under way was so much a factor in our postpresidential lives— it is part of the story of this book.

Including the presidential library and museum, our offices and projects, the center is built on the hill from which General William

Tecumseh Sherman watched the battle of Atlanta and commands a beautiful view of the skyline of the city that has risen from the ashes he left. With its low round buildings, understated in design and beautiful, it is everything we wanted it to be. The library houses the records of the Carter presidency and is an immediately accessible resource for scholars and leaders; the museum is a place where visitors of all ages and nationalities can learn about the history of our country from the perspective of its first thirty-nine presidents; and the Carter Center offers a place for study, research, and action on issues of importance to America and other nations of the world.

In one of the most peculiar laws of our land, applicable since the time of George Washington to the day we left the White House, all the correspondence, records, documents, and mementos of a presidency belonged personally to the president. In the early days of the country the volume was relatively small and could be hauled in a wagon or two to the ex-president's home. Many of these precious documents were lost—destroyed by fire, rodents, moisture, or insects or sold by destitute or mercenary heirs to autograph merchants. In more recent years, in order to preserve the history of our nation, a law was passed that provided for presidents to raise funds from private contributions for the construction of a library to house the documents and, once built, to deed the facility to the government.

On January 20, 1981, when we left Washington and flew to Plains on Air Force One, twenty-one tractor trailers loaded with records and mementos followed us to Georgia. They were unloaded and stored in the old post office building in Atlanta, and a staff of professional archivists immediately began working on them. They soon estimated that after screening the files, there would remain 27 million documents that would be valuable to students, historians, biographers, and other scholars.

ROSALYNN
> The buildings of the center are futuristic in appearance—but with classical columns—and blend artfully into the topography of the site. Two

small lakes separate the heavily visited library-museum and the more isolated and scholarly environment of the Carter Center. One of our most prized gifts is a beautiful Japanese garden between the lakes, donated by the Tadao Yoshida family, longtime friends in Japan. It was designed by Kinsaku Nakane, one of that country's "national treasures," who personally placed every one of the seven hundred tons of stone to create nineteen feet of waterfalls and the garden, which he then filled with masses of azaleas and other native plants.

Across the lakes from the library is where, as Jimmy has often said, "we will probably spend the rest of our active lives" working on issues that are important to our country and the world.

JIMMY
As governor and president, I learned—sometimes the hard way— about the need for thorough study of an issue before presenting it to the public or taking specific action. Bringing leaders together who are both knowledgeable and have authority to act is one of the best ways to deal with problems. Often, however, it is difficult for incompatible leaders to meet in an official capacity. Private or academic experts can make the analyses, but the recommendations that come out of such sessions are usually deposited on library shelves and never reach those who are able to act. We hoped to be able to overcome some of these difficulties with a degree of activism along with the scholarly studies, and began our work even before we had our own facilities.

From the beginning we wanted to be sure that the center was not regarded as partisan, and former President Gerald Ford has been co-chairman with me on three of our major consultations: Middle East peace; U.S.-Soviet relations, including arms control; and democracy in Latin America.

Each of these consultations has been conducted over a period of a year or more. They have brought together internationally recognized experts who have done much of the preliminary work, and the findings have then been shared with those most concerned, including administration leaders in Washington, key members of Congress, and interested heads of foreign governments. Since these are continuing projects, we have chosen senior scholars, or "fellows," to work at the center on the subjects, which also include human rights, global health care, the environment, and conflict resolution.

Our studies have revealed what can happen when people of directly opposing views meet together to discuss problems. In the session culminating our Middle East study, for instance, we had representatives from Israel, Syria, Lebanon, Saudi Arabia, Jordan, and Egypt, along with Palestinians. It was the first time many of them had ever met face-to-face. There were some sharp exchanges, but no one ever walked out and the debates were not marked by personal vituperation. Sometimes they would not speak directly to each other, but would relay their messages by addressing the chair. Nevertheless, they communicated freely even on the most controversial issues. Although basic differences remained, it was surprising how much these officials and scholars were able to agree before the week was over, and we were struck by the potential for peace even in that volatile area. We longed for the day when the heads of state could participate in similar free discussions with a genuine desire for progress and a modicum of political courage.

JIMMY

Although some efforts were made by one or two Middle Eastern leaders to reopen peace talks, no one was ready to provide the kind of leadership needed at that time. Still, all genuine progress in important matters builds on small steps taken in the past.

After the consultation I wrote a book, *The Blood of Abraham*, published in 1985, about the history, current situation and possible future of the Middle East. It has a chapter on each of the major players, describing as best I could the particular attitudes, arguments, and hopes as seen from within each country.

Similarly, a study on U.S.-Soviet relations in 1984 and 1985 brought about some interesting results. Again working closely with President Ford, we were joined by most of the American officials who had conducted arms-control negotiations for the past fifteen years, including three former secretaries of state, national security advisers, secretaries of defense, leaders from both houses of Congress, and other specialists. Delegations came from the nations with nuclear weapons— France, Great Britain, China, and the Soviet Union—and others from countries that have at least the technical capability of producing nuclear explosives, including Israel, Japan, Canada, East and West Germany, Argentina, Brazil, Pakistan, and India.

The Soviets, participating in small working groups all week and in the large plenary sessions at the end, demonstrated a surprising flexibility that was subsequently made official by General Secretary Mikhail Gorbachev himself. For the first time they expressed a willingness to stop nuclear testing and to permit on-site inspection of some of their facilities if necessary to resolve arguments about compliance with existing agreements.

When this consultation began, there were no plans for a final statement from the participants, but before it was over, with so many areas of agreement, everyone wanted to have a set of recommendations drawn up. It was done with practically unanimous consent, providing a good outline of how past agreements could be honored and how future negotiations could be successful. Again, the results were widely disseminated within our own nation and among scholars, scientists, and political leaders in many other countries.

The consultation on Latin America was of a different nature, bringing together more than a dozen incumbent or former heads of state of democratic nations in the region and attempting to reach as much understanding as possible on such important questions as: What makes it possible for a democracy to be born and to replace a totalitarian government of the left or right? What are the greatest dangers to the survival of a newborn or youthful democracy? Because of an upsurge in demands for freedom and human rights, a number of democracies have emerged or reemerged in recent years in countries such as Peru, Argentina, Brazil, Uruguay, and Ecuador, and these questions were acutely pertinent to the assembled leaders. They discussed the intervention of foreign powers, terrorism, human rights violations, heavy debt

burdens, distribution of land and other resources, excessive urbanization, homelessness, unemployment, and poverty. They made it plain that
when parents with starving children are forced to choose between bread
and liberty, they are at least tempted to accept an authoritarian regime
that promises quick alleviation of their suffering. It helps, of course, for
a society to have enjoyed a heritage of human rights and democratic principles of government. The absence of such a history is a destabilizing
force, and we sought answers to how such countries can make that
difficult beginning toward a more progressive government. The leaders
learned a lot from one another and were able to strengthen their individual and concerted efforts to preserve freedom in our hemisphere.

We do not, of course, expect instant change to result from these
consultations, but believe that by bringing opposing groups together
for free and open discussion, all sides can gain a better understanding
of the issues and perhaps find ways to approach one another more
easily in the future.

On another front, we have extended the "Closing the Gap" analyses to global health problems, to cover the infectious and contagious
diseases and illnesses caused by malnutrition that are no longer as
prevalent in the United States as in some other countries. The programs
resulting from these studies are some of our most exciting. We had
already begun a project called Global 2000, to help small farmers in
Africa and Asia increase their food production, and now we have
expanded that to include preventive health measures. Among the same
farm families we are beginning to study nutrition and disease, the
number of births in a family, the number of babies that die, the spacing
of children, and other information that will be helpful in determining
the health needs of the people.

We are also working closely with the Task Force for Child Survival
and Development, a joint effort of national and international organizations to immunize all the world's children and to teach parents oral rehydration therapy for the treatment of diarrhea. Dr. Bill Foege, the Carter
Center Health Fellow, is also executive director of this task force. In

discussing diarrheal diseases, which are the most prevalent killer of small children in the Third World, Dr. Foege says that possibly the greatest medical development of the decade, a simple cure for diarrhea, has been found—one teaspoon of sugar and one-quarter teaspoon of salt dissolved in an eight-ounce glass of water. Despite its almost miraculous effectiveness, the mixture is not the panacea that one would think, because it takes education for it to be effective. Mothers have to be taught, in the first place, to give liquid to their babies that have diarrhea, and they must also be careful to mix the ingredients with clean water.

JIMMY

I was eager to begin to develop one of the vital components of our original plan for the center: studying the principles of conflict resolution based upon my own experiences and the vast amount of scholarly work that has been done in this field in recent years. The need is obvious not only in disputes between nations but also in resolving other disagreements. Conflict resolution will be an increasingly important part of our work at the Carter Center.

Our first case, to test the techniques we are developing, dealt with a domestic issue—tobacco. We brought together people on both sides of the issue: on the one hand, tobacco growers, officials from tobacco-producing states, representatives of tobacco organizations, a spokesman for the smokeless tobacco industry, and on the other, leaders of health organizations, experts from the Centers for Disease Control, and the heads of doctors' organizations. And before the three-day meeting was over they actually managed to agree on a few key points, usually for completely different reasons of self-interest. Both sides wanted to maintain tight restrictions on the acreage of tobacco grown in this country, minimize imports of foreign tobacco, and maintain high market prices for the leaf. Even though the farmers grew tobacco for a living, most of them favored the prohibition of advertising that appealed to teenagers and were as determined as the doctors that their own children not smoke.

Ideally, we will be offering our facilities regularly for all manner of direct talks, mediation, or arbitration to opposing parties who have a disagreement they cannot resolve by themselves. It wouldn't be appropriate for the Carter Center to attempt to represent our nation in any way or to interfere with normal diplomatic efforts. However, under certain conditions disagreeing parties could spend a few days together, perhaps with a trusted mediator, and at least be able to communicate without the danger of embarrassment on either side. They would be provided a quiet and secluded place and, on occasion, the meetings could be held in secrecy. It might even be appropriate in some instances to help arrange such sessions outside the United States.

Another continuing role for the center will be to work with human rights organizations, to honor the most courageous and effective foes of persecution, to publicize abuses and, when appropriate, to intercede directly and try to persuade oppressive leaders to alleviate the suffering of their people.

We have come to know some wonderful, compassionate, and concerned people who have helped to make it possible for us to pursue the causes we think are important. Through the generosity of Dominique de Menil of Houston, Texas, we have established the Carter/Menil Award for Human Rights. This prize, including one hundred thousand dollars in cash, is being presented on occasion to one or two people or organizations that have been the most courageous and effective in working to expose and protest human rights abuses. Imagine how pleased we were when several months after we chose him as our first recipient, we learned that the founder of the Moscow-based Helsinki Watch Group, Yuri Orlov, would be released after a decade in prison and exile on the very day we were to announce the award. I was able to tell him the good news first hand as soon as he arrived in the United States. Our hope is that publicity about the selections will increase awareness of the abuses that are still so common in many lands.

ROSALYNN

I am playing an active role in all the projects of the Carter Center. I have been especially pleased to be able to continue my interest in mental health, with a series of four annual seminars. The first one dealt with the stigma attached to mental illnesses, which we will continue to pursue; the second one, with financing services. My hope is to bring together the disparate groups concerned about mental health issues to go on developing common priorities.

It has become increasingly apparent that the issues in which we are involved are of wide concern, and from our experience we have learned that many people want to help.

In the years while Jimmy was president, hundreds of thousands of starving and sick Cambodians fled the war and persecution in their homeland, either in fragile boats heading out to sea or across minefields on the borders into Thailand. I went to Thailand to see for myself their desperate plight and to report back to Jimmy and the American people about what we could do to help. The outpouring of financial and personal support for the Cambodians far exceeded anything we had ever anticipated.

More recently, we have seen how people in America and across the world have joined in various ways to help feed the hungry, especially in Africa. Student movements were formed on college campuses to oppose apartheid in South Africa, and their voices were heard not only by college trustees but also in corporate boardrooms and the halls of Congress. There can be no doubt that peace demonstrations in Europe helped to bring about the resumption of Soviet-American arms talks. Some of these efforts by ordinary citizens have generated large sums for worthy causes, but, perhaps even more important, they have aroused public interest so that those in positions of influence have been forced to pay attention to the issues. This shows us that ordinary individuals can make a difference on great world issues.

JIMMY

Before my father died, my mother confined her interests to nursing and being a good mother and housewife, but she was too strong and lively a woman to live a lonely, sedentary life with her children grown and her husband gone. She first became a fraternity house mother at Auburn University, then organized and managed a nursing home for the elderly, but came back to Plains because she got tired of being around "old people," and was looking for something else to do.

At age sixty-eight, she was watching television one evening and saw a public service advertisement for the Peace Corps: "Is your glass half empty, or is it half full?" It got her attention, but what she noticed most was the statement "Age is no barrier." The next morning she sent off for an application, and then came to the warehouse office and informed Billy and me that she was joining the Peace Corps and wanted to go either to Africa or to India. She was somewhat taken aback when we were neither surprised nor opposed and merely replied, "Okay, Mama, if that's what you want to do."

She was selected without delay, and trained for service in India. The most difficult task for her was to learn a new language well enough to carry out her duties. She was assigned to implement a family planning program in a small village near Bombay, and managed the local dialect well enough to get by. Walking on the narrow footpaths between homes, she explained the advantages of limited families to doubtful parents, and later put on puppet shows for larger audiences, making her points through the dramatic exclamations of the small figures she had created.

But she was uncomfortable with the forced vasectomies and the intense pressure put on young couples to limit their families to two children. Being a registered nurse, she managed to get a job as a volunteer in the local clinic after her regular working hours. She soon became indispensable to the doctor, who requested that she work full time with him in treating the two or three hundred patients who came to the clinic every day. Back in Plains, we were deluged with her requests for vaccines to immunize the children and medicine to treat leprosy, infections, typhoid fever, and other diseases of the area.

It was fulfilling work for her under difficult conditions. When we learned by "reading between the lines" that she was hungry, we began sending her boxes of food—which she gave away to those hungrier than she was. After two years in India she came home. She was weak and tired and weighed forty-four pounds less than when she left. Exhausted by the trip home, she had to leave the airplane in a wheelchair—to her great embarrassment. She didn't have a dime and had had to borrow some coins from a redcap to store her luggage during a long layover in the Shannon airport in Ireland.

ROSALYNN

There was a small news item when Miss Lillian returned, because by then Jimmy was an active candidate for governor, but she soon became a celebrity in her own right because of her humor and the exciting stories about what she had seen and done. After she regained her strength, she made many speeches and appearances on radio and television talk shows, promoting the Peace Corps, encouraging volunteerism, and making fun of the all-too-common belief that the age of seventy should bring the end of an active and exciting life.

In our travels we have found American volunteers in the second half of their lives serving in some unlikely places. Recently we visited El Salvador and found the capital city almost like an armed camp. San Salvador had the tightest security we have ever seen, with the possible exception of Beirut, in war-torn Lebanon. We scheduled a meeting at the U.S. embassy residence with some of the Salvadoran leaders to learn what we could about the economy, the status of human rights violations, and the political situation. To our surprise, among those invited by the ambassador were two old friends, Bobby and Erlene Smith. We had first known them through the Georgia Crop Improvement Association when Bobby was growing and processing cottonseed and we were doing the same with peanuts. A popular and successful businessman, he later served as under secretary of agriculture while we were in Washington.

We thought Bobby had retired.

"I have," he told us. "Erlene and I have been here for a few months working in a program for retired business executives, called the International Executive Service Corps (IESC). The Salvadoran people have some problems with cotton production and marketing, and we volunteered to help them find some solutions."

He explained that all cotton grown in the country is ginned and marketed through a cotton cooperative, an organization of growers and ginners. His specific duty was to help them find a way to improve the efficiency of their operations. He visited the different gins, or "plantels," in the country, studied their production, harvesting, and processing techniques, and made suggestions for improvements based on his own experience.

Guerrilla attacks were constantly interrupting electrical power, so Bobby helped secure a large diesel generator to provide emergency power for the gins. He also helped settle a controversy between the cooperative and Mexican buyers. The dispute concerned the quality of the cotton, and after unsuccessful negotiation attempts, Bobby arranged for a qualified USDA inspector to take a leave of absence and come to examine the bales. His decision went against the Salvadorans, but at least the impasse was ended.

While Bobby was doing this work, another retired executive from Lubbock, Texas, was reorganizing the cooperative's bookkeeping system and office. Both men were working as volunteers for the IESC. The nonprofit organization was founded in 1964 to match retired business men and women to companies in the developing world. About nine thousand retirees are available to serve for no salary, but are paid travel and per diem expenses. Spouses often join in the project or help in other ways. While the executive works in the host company, her husband might teach English in a local school.

After successes overseas, an associated organization, the National Executives Service Corps (NESC) began addressing problems at home by placing retired executives with nonprofit organizations in this country. Today nonprofits are generally short of manpower or money or both. (We know this is true for the Carter Center.) As a result, most have problems they cannot address properly without some outside help. On one assignment the retired president of a large corporation helped a struggling college reduce its operating costs by 25 percent. On another, an expert in painting and plant maintenance still shares his skills with ex-prisoners enrolled in a job training program.

NESC volunteers often go to great lengths to accommodate their clients. We have a dynamo friend, Jeno Paulucci, founder of Jeno's Pizza and Chun King Frozen Foods, who has flown many thousands of miles at his own expense to help the Oglala Sioux Indians in South Dakota improve production of their manufacturing plant. For over two years he worked with the Indians, first to get rid of a staggering $2 million debt, and then to redefine their manufacturing and marketing strategy. Next he helped them get a large contract from the Defense Department to manufacture leather gloves, arranged for funds to purchase the equipment, and helped make contacts with prospective customers. It has been quite a saga of one dedicated volunteer spending his own time, money, and energy battling the bureaucracy to help get jobs for American Indians living in one of the poorest regions in the United States. He keeps going back because, like many Americans in the second half of their lives, he has found that helping others with difficult jobs "you couldn't pay me to do" is an exciting challenge.

Although Carter's Warehouse was not a nonprofit organization, we learned at first hand how important a management consultant can be. We received a Small Business Administration loan when we were struggling to expand our business, and took advantage of a special program the agency offered that was similar to that of the NESC. We had just moved into new offices, added a cotton gin and begun to process cotton for farmers in addition to our peanut business, and wanted to be sure we had an efficient operation. The Atlanta business executive who helped us had suffered a heart attack while still relatively young and had had to retire, but he was still using his management skills to aid others— and to us the service was invaluable.

Norman Borlaug is another of those people who retired, though not at a young age, and is still using his skills to help others. Dr. Borlaug won the Nobel Peace Prize in 1970 for helping to bring about the Green Revolution in India and Pakistan. Along with a team of agricultural scientists he worked with farmers on small plots of land to teach them how to increase their food production. India now not only produces enough grain to feed its people but also exports large quantities.

After more than forty years of overseas work in breeding more productive strains of wheat and corn, Dr. Borlaug officially retired so that he could return to the United States with his wife and take a semi-active position on the faculty of Texas A & M University. After a lifetime of dedicated service he could have rested on his laurels. But the Norman Borlaug we know could not have done this. Now past the age of seventy, he is working on many important projects around the world. He is an original sponsor and now the senior adviser for our Global 2000 project, working with us to bring about a "green revolution" in several countries in southern Asia and the sub-Saharan region of Africa. He helped us recruit agricultural scientists to serve in these nations, and because of their experience and dedicated work the early results of this program have far exceeded our expectations. We hope that in six or eight years there will be a permanent improvement in food production in these famine-stricken areas.

Another special friend who has been adapting impressively to changing needs for a long time is Esther Peterson, who in her gentle way is a formidable force. With a silver braid coiled around her head and blue eyes brimming with warmth and enthusiasm, Esther looks like a model for a Norman Rockwell portrait of the ideal grandmother, except that she carries a briefcase. Her grandchildren would testify that she is the ideal grandmother, briefcase and all, but she is also more. Esther has been fighting for the rights of underdogs for more than half a century.

Unlikely as it may seem, it was a Valentine heart that first got her involved in helping others. She was a young recreation worker in a poor neighborhood, where many of the women were seamstresses, making aprons. Their employer gave an order that henceforth the pockets on the aprons would be heart shaped, rather than the usual squares. Heart-shaped pockets took more time to sew on, but the women would be required to produce the same number of aprons for the same pay. Esther joined the fight for more pay for the Valentine pockets, and she has been fighting unfairness ever since in the workplace, the marketplace, and the church, or through the government at any level. She became a good friend of Eleanor Roosevelt and has worked tirelessly under several Democratic presidents.

JIMMY

> Esther served as my special assistant for consumer affairs. One of her pet projects was to bring an end to the dumping in Third World nations of dangerous products banned in this country. Tris was the catalyst that brought long-held concerns to the forefront. When this product that made children's clothes flameproof was shown to cause cancer in animals, the product was banned and unsold stocks were withdrawn from the market. The manufacturers were also required to recall garments that had been sold and make refunds. Some companies tried to recoup their losses by dumping unsold Tris-treated garments in Third World nations that lacked regulations to protect their children. Esther successfully confronted this one-shot scandal, but she knew that the dumping of pharmaceuticals and pesticides banned in our country was an ongoing tragedy. Based on her research and recommendations, I issued an executive order in January 1981 aimed at ending such practices.

When President Reagan rescinded the order early in his first term, Esther Peterson was crushed but not defeated. She found a different forum—the United Nations. She became the accredited representative, without pay, of an organization of consumer groups from fifty countries. In this capacity she induced the United Nations to establish a list of banned and severely restricted products from all nations. Written in simple layman's language that officials without specialized technical training can understand, the list is maintained and now includes information on nearly five hundred products from sixty nations. Esther has struck another blow for the right to safety for people all over the world.

When she called to tell us that she had been asked to speak at the First International Conference of Consumerism in Latin America to be held in Uruguay on the same day as the formal opening of the Carter Center, we were disappointed that she would not be there to share our celebration, but urged her to go to Uruguay and continue her fight. Though in her eighties, Esther Peterson is still a force to be reckoned with, despite her disarming grandmotherly smile.

The Friendship Force is an organization that is very special to us. It has grown from one man's vision and dedication to become a force for better understanding among the peoples of the world. During the early 1970s, while we were in the governor's mansion, a Presbyterian minister named Wayne Smith came home to Atlanta after serving as a missionary in Brazil for seven years. He was so enthusiastic about the country that he wanted everyone to know and love it as he did.

At about the same time, we were planning a trip to several Latin American countries to find new markets for Georgia products. Wayne heard that we were going and offered to be our guide and interpreter. Our trade efforts were successful, and we had a wonderful time during a brief stop in Pernambuco, Brazil, which happened to be Georgia's sister state.

At Wayne's suggestion we decided to arrange an exchange between the citizens of Atlanta and Recife, the capitals of our two states. He did most of the work, and within a few months a planeload of Georgians, more than two hundred, flew to Recife, and the same plane brought a load of Brazilians back to Atlanta.

All the travelers were required to find a family in their own city to be hosts for one of the foreign guests during the ten-day exchange visit. Our rules were that visitors must spend half the time in the home provided, and then could travel at their own expense. But it was such an enjoyable experience to stay in a private home that almost no one did any independent traveling. The fact that few in either group spoke any foreign language turned out to be not much of a barrier. Everyone got along well by using sign language and a smattering of new words that they quickly learned. There were a lot of tears at the airports on departure day, and it was not long before the host families became the visitors.

We arranged a similar trip every year we were in Atlanta, with several required study sessions on the customs and traditions of the country before each trip. Whenever possible, people were placed with families who had similar occupations—farmers with farmers, teachers with teachers, and policemen with policemen. (In those early days a traveler could participate for only two hundred dollars to cover the cost of air travel.) That was the origin of the Friendship Force.

ROSALYNN

After the successful 1976 presidential election, Wayne Smith came to see us with a suggestion for a greatly expanded program. During our first month in the White House, Jimmy explained the concept to the nation's governors, and a number of them decided to join in the program. Wayne, retired from a first career, agreed to be the full-time director, and I have been honorary chairperson ever since.

Under Wayne's leadership the program has mushroomed. We now have chapters in forty-two states and more than forty foreign countries, with annual meetings in such places as Rio de Janeiro, Bangkok, Munich, and Tokyo, attended by several hundred volunteers who coordinate the program in their various countries. More than three hundred thousand people have already participated in these exchanges, and other nations have taken the initiative to organize visits among themselves that no longer involve the United States.

The Friendship Force is open to anyone, and although travel costs have increased since those early days, it is still a bargain because of the hospitality of host families. Our motto is "A world of friends is a world of peace." We believe that breaking down cultural and language barriers, and getting to know and understand people of other nations, can lead to a more peaceful world. A nonprofit organization supported only by private contributions, the Friendship Force opens avenues of communication and understanding that transcend political boundaries and help to heal past wounds and ease existing tensions. We call our travelers "ambassadors" and perhaps Wayne Smith—just one man with vision—should be named an international "minister of peace."

These are stories of people who are using the second half of their lives in meaningful ways, and activities such as these are open to all of us. There are many programs—some well known, others not—that offer us a chance to reach out to the world. Whatever our skills and experience, there is always something we can do.

One of the best-known overseas programs, of course, is the Peace Corps. It is still a wonderful opportunity for those who want extended overseas service. If one is more specifically concerned about housing the poor in a Third World country, Habitat for Humanity can always use help from volunteers willing to serve for three years. Other opportunities require commitments of one, two, or three years. Programs such as Wycliffe Bible Translators welcome doctors and dentists, who travel at their own expense, usually carrying medical supplies and equipment donated by firms or groups, to care for people in remote villages. There are many needs for teachers, especially those who are fluent in other languages, and even more opportunities that require only willingness to work on construction and archaeological digs, or with children or disabled people. In the past, such activities were aimed almost entirely at younger adults, but more and more groups are seeking senior workers as well. Agricultural projects range from Israeli kibbutzim to raspberry picking in Scotland, or, for those with strong commitment, helping with the coffee and cotton harvests in Nicaragua. These require long hours of hard physical labor in exchange for a chance to visit foreign places over an extended period of time.

Volunteers who cannot sign up for these long-term commitments can still serve abroad. Many churches provide programs for short-term service, either as a member of a group or as an individual volunteer. When we were members of the Northside Drive Baptist Church in Atlanta, a team of doctors, nurses, and young people from our congregation went every summer to some isolated community in Central

America or the Caribbean to provide health services. For one month they worked among the people, giving physical examinations, medical treatment, and dental care. Our son Chip went on one of the summer trips and helped to vaccinate children.

The small Methodist Church congregation in Plains regularly sends a group to Haiti to help build churches and schools—and these are not trained carpenters but ordinary church members, men and women, young and old.

In a typical year some sixty-eight hundred volunteers go abroad under the auspices of the Southern Baptist Convention for periods of two weeks to six months. Most other church groups offer similar opportunities. When we travel to foreign countries, we try to meet with volunteers from different denominations, many of whom work together as partners in order to be more effective and in some cases to protect themselves from political harassment.

The Mennonites have a long tradition of moving teams into an area to help in an emergency, both in the United States and abroad, and other denominations like ours are beginning to join them.

Other programs, such as Sister Cities and Partners of the Americas, offer opportunities for working together with distant communities as well as exchanges for educational purposes. Also, Sister Cities provides a chance to help a poorer "sister" in various essential areas: firefighting, solid-waste management, agricultural development, combating infectious diseases, setting up training centers for building trades, public-health nursing, and vehicle repair. When disaster strikes, the sister ties are used as avenues for quickly channeling needed aid to suffering people.

Those who cannot participate in travel exchanges and seminars or programs like Sister Cities can still have direct involvement with people from other cultures. One good way is through the Christmas International House, an interdenominational program that matches international students with families in the United States over the two-week holiday period. Usually at least ten families in a community provide holiday homes for students so that they can plan some joint activities. Salunga, Pennsylvania, a Mennonite farming community, hosted one hundred students from around the world over Christmas in 1985. Sadly, though many students were placed in homes in communities all over the United States under the program, another six hundred had to be turned away because not enough homes were available.

After we established diplomatic relations with China, we launched an extensive exchange program for students, and now there are more than fifteen thousand Chinese scholars studying in American universities, mostly at the graduate level. Many of these and of the other 360,000 international students who are studying in the United States will be future world leaders. Sharing holidays with some of them is not only an enjoyable way to learn more about other countries from eager young people, but it is also a means of showing them how Americans really live and makes their holidays a warm experience instead of a lonely one.

There is an opportunity to fit almost everyone's interest, but there is a special element that must be considered in deciding what to do in one's later years. Not everyone wants to go to a distant community or a foreign country or be involved on a regular basis in volunteer activity. Retirement years should be enjoyable, and there are many interesting ways to expand our minds about international or national issues and be helpful without traveling away from home.

Many colleges and museums offer programs of study, and even the smallest libraries usually have a wealth of materials, including video cassette documentaries and programs that one can watch on home television. Returning participants in various travel seminars will often speak at civic clubs, schools, and churches. Former and current government officials may be available for providing background information; returning diplomats, missionaries, and Peace Corps volunteers are also resources for those who may not be able to go abroad but wish to delve deeper than the evening news.

For those who would like to participate in human rights activities, one especially effective and worthy effort is made by Amnesty International, which works to stop torture and to obtain the release of prisoners of conscience who have not used or advocated violence. Anyone can join the thousands of members who stay informed about human rights abuses and become involved in actively seeking the release of a particular prisoner by focusing public attention on the case, writing to the oppressive leaders, or influencing public officials to take an active interest in the prisoner. Other human rights groups that monitor and bring attention to such problems include Helsinki Watch, Americas Watch, and the Lawyers Committee on Human Rights. We are working with all of these organizations at the Carter Center.

The most convenient and immediate way to help any organization is by making a financial contribution. Those concerned about the poor in Third World countries can make a contribution to Habitat for Humanity so that "someone who goes barefoot that you will never see," as one of our Uganda friends told us, "can have a home to live in." Less than ten dollars a week for a year can build a Habitat home for ten people in India, Uganda, or Central America. A few dollars to CARE, Catholic Charities, or the humanitarian arm of other religious groups, and to nonsectarian organizations, such as the Child Survival Task Force, can provide important food and medical aid. Immunization against six preventable childhood diseases for a child in a Third World country costs less than ten dollars, and oral rehydration kits are produced for only a few cents.

Contributions are critical to good causes. We know, because we have spent a lot of time trying to raise money for some of them ourselves, and we can assure you that every amount, no matter how large or small, is important and appreciated.

Each of us can help, in our own special ways, with the needs of our fellow citizens around the world. Just as surely as there is a place for service in our own communities, there is a way for us to use our minds, our convictions, and our political beliefs, and to get involved in important issues on a national and international level. There are wonderful outlets for anyone who is interested and willing to expand his or her involvement beyond the duties of family and a regular career. And for those, like us, who have reached retirement age, the opportunities are boundless.

No matter how much or how little we have accomplished in the first part of our lives, it is never too late for unprecedented experiences. The second half of our lives can actually be a time of greater risk-taking for those of us whose responsibilities may have left little room for taking chances before—not foolish or pointless risks, but risks that offer the hope of both real adventure and real reward, for ourselves and others. While some of our physical powers may be diminished, we have survival skills younger people may not have learned, a different kind of endurance that comes with the passage of time.

As the title of this book says, we have nothing to lose and everything to gain. Whether it is the awkwardness of trying to twist our tongues around a new language or the physical challenge of keeping our bodies in shape, we have lost some of our youthful self-consciousness. We have been laughed at before and survived. We have been hurt, lonely, disappointed, defeated before, and survived. There is no longer any danger that we will cut off a promising career before it has begun.

But we do have something we never had before: we have the added pressure of time. We can no longer wait around for the ideal opportunity. If we have not achieved our early dreams, we must either find new ones or see what we can salvage from the old. If we have accomplished what we set out to do in our youth, then we need not weep like Alexander the Great that we have no more worlds to conquer. There is clearly much left to be done, and whatever else we are going to do, we had better get on with it.

We and the World

Mountain climbers climb mountains for the same reason I go around them. They are there.

—Jimmy Townsend

Jimmy

We flew low over the Magdalena River, 120 miles northwest of Bogotá, Colombia, and twenty-five miles east of the snowcapped Nevada del Ruiz volcano. I was seated just behind the helicopter pilots and leaned forward as we approached the tributary river Lagunilla. There below us was a vast sea of mud surrounding a few isolated buildings perched on top of a small hill. When Ruiz had erupted a few days earlier, November 13, 1985, its permanent snow and ice cover melted and the resulting torrents of water carried millions of tons of pumice and rocks down the stream beds of the rivers and into the populated valley.

"That is only five percent of the town of Armero," the pilot said. "The rest of the homes, stores, warehouses, vehicles, animals, and people were covered and carried away by a towering wall of mud. It was one hundred fifty feet deep in some of the canyons upstream and as high as a six-story building when it reached this town. We were able to locate and rescue only a few hundred people who were trapped. The government had just completed a census in this area a few weeks before the disaster, so we know that more than twenty thousand people are still buried, including eight thousand children. They will never be found."

After its initial devastating rush, the hot mixture of pumice, water, and debris had slowly spread out over a wider area below the stricken village, carrying some of its victims several miles downstream. On the hillsides and in the remaining trees we could see how deep the mud had once been. Entire houses, trees, and tractor-trailer trucks were piled high against immovable natural obstacles. Although most of the dead animals on the surface had been removed to reduce the chance of disease from their rotting bodies, a few were unreachable and still exposed. The stench reached up to us, several hundred feet above the surface.

I had come to Colombia at the request of President Belisario Betancur Cuartas and UNICEF, of which I am honorary chairman of the U.S. Committee. We were attempting to prevent the spread of disease among the fifty thousand homeless people left in the area and to assist in the final stages of a remarkable immunization program in the country. On this single day the goal was to vaccinate five hundred thousand prospective mothers and an equal number of young children.

Early in the morning President Betancur and I had administered Sabin polio vaccine to two baby boys in a televised ceremony at the presidential palace. Then the president joined Roman Catholic Cardinal Trujillo in an airborne funeral service for the volcano's victims, which was broadcast to the nation while their plane circled high above the massive burial grounds. In the meantime, Colombia's First Lady, Doña Rosa Helena, and I were en route to three villages in the disaster area, where medical specialists, trained Red Cross volunteers, and hundreds of women and children were waiting for us.

In temporary "hospitals" we found survivors from Armero first in line. I was impressed by their stoic acceptance of the recent tragedy and the obvious communal love for the small children. All of us felt that these few little ones were exceptionally precious.

One infant girl in the village of Mariquita was held by a man. I asked him about the child's mother, and he replied, "She is lost, with all our other children. My mother and father were also killed, as were my only brother and two sisters. My baby girl and I are the only ones left in my family." It was an emotional moment for me, and when I asked if he wished to return someday to Armero, he replied, *"No, nunca. Todos mis recuerdos son malos"* (No, never. All my memories are bad).

Under Betancur's leadership, Colombia became a pioneer in child health care. Beginning early in 1984, more than a hundred thousand volunteers were mobilized and trained to serve at ten thousand vaccination posts. The mass media joined the campaign, as did many religious and civic groups, including policemen and teachers. On the Sundays before vaccination days, the sermons in all 2,280 parishes of Colombia were dedicated to the subject. More than eight hundred thousand children—85 percent of the total—had been immunized. Now a much broader campaign had been adopted to monitor children's growth, promote breast-feeding, distribute oral rehydration packets for the treatment of diarrhea, and to educate the public on the opportunities for improving the survival of children. Other nations around the world were being encouraged to follow the example of Colombia, and I needed to see what was being done.

Although this particular trip was in response to an extraordinary tragedy, several times each year we travel to different places around the world, usually in conjunction with work at the Carter Center.

No matter what prompts us to make a trip, we have learned over the years to broaden its purpose as much as possible. Sometimes we have specific obligations related to our work—meetings with foreign officials or with organizations and people involved in benevolent causes. But self-education is another reason for travel, even for former first families. After careful study at home, foreign visits are often the only way to understand a complicated subject. In effect, we "go to school" for a while among a wide range of people who are the most knowledgeable and experienced in various fields.

Other travel is for the sheer enjoyment of it. Even when there are official or business duties to perform, we now take extra time to venture out on our own, to see the sights, and to enjoy the people and places we visit. There are advantages to being private citizens!

Everyone needs some relaxation, a chance to get away from the pressures of work or the responsibilities or boredom of day-to-day activities. Travel can provide that for us. While we all can enjoy our visits, the real challenge is to derive as much benefit from them as possible and maybe contribute something to others in the process. In doing so, we are likely to have surprisingly varied and rich encounters that would otherwise be impossible.

Although travel can sometimes be a hassle with all the packing, plane schedules, and unexpected minor problems, we cannot imagine a rounded life without it. Among other benefits, travel gives us a chance to gain perspective on our life at home. There is nothing like being away for a while to give us the ability to look back objectively to measure the values of what we are doing. From a distance it is easier to make a few resolutions about more effective use of time and energy when we return. If we plan our trips well, we can almost always expand our own professional knowledge or personal interests.

JIMMY

For instance, while on my trip to Colombia, I was intrigued by a program being used in the hospitals of Bogotá that was based upon ancient Indian customs and designed to save the lives of premature babies. The new technique offers wonderful possibilities for Colombia and other undeveloped countries that cannot afford expensive incubators and extended hospital care for more than a few of these children. (In some countries as high as 50 to 70 percent of all babies are born underweight.)

Minister of Health Rafael de Zubiria explained the new development. "We call the system *cangaru* [kangaroo]. It needs no technology and its cost is practically zero. Instead of being placed in incubators, the abnormally small babies are strapped close to their mothers, under the sweaters or blouses and between the breasts. Each baby's temperature is maintained uniformly by the mother's body heat, and the infant can feed throughout the day from both breasts, taking small amounts of milk as needed. From their mothers the babies acquire immunization from infection, relative freedom from diarrhea and constipation, and the psychological advantage of constant intimacy. As soon as possible, usually within a day, the mother and child are sent home, though the baby will remain strapped close until a certain safe weight is achieved."

The minister added that the results of the system compared favorably with the use of incubators in more advanced societies and had been dramatic in Colombia. He believes the same thing can happen in even the most isolated rural areas when health workers can train new mothers to be "kangaroo" mothers.

A few months later, at a Carter Center global health consultation, we invited Colombia's health minister to describe this new procedure for premature babies to the assembled delegates from many nations. It was here that we resolved to add information about *cangaru* mothers to the Child Survival Task Force program.

Although no incumbent president ever traveled outside our national borders until this century, it is undeniable that foreign travel can give a president important opportunities to understand and communicate with leaders of other nations and to make friends for the United States abroad. All of our trips were memorable, but little about them would qualify as pleasure. Almost every minute was carefully scheduled, with extensive briefings from American diplomats in the foreign capital, long official meetings with our hosts, elaborate receptions and banquets, and ceremonial visits to veterans' memorials or children's hospitals. Even at events designed primarily for our enjoyment, we were so heavily covered by the press that what we saw most often was a sea of U.S. secret service agents, foreign security officers, and dozens of television cameras and flashbulbs. Though we were usually able to get in some early-morning jogging in special secluded places, there was little chance for any impromptu activities, private moments, or genuine encounters with average citizens of a country.

We still have tightly scheduled meetings when we travel, but since leaving the White House we have been able to combine our necessary business with a lot more pleasure. We can make last-minute changes in our itinerary, and spend more time in remote areas.

We have our choice of staying with personal friends, in native or Western-style hotels, or in one of the country's guesthouses. On a rare occasion when there might be special security problems, as in

El Salvador in 1986, we have stayed in the American ambassador's residence. In general, however, we prefer to stay as close as possible to the people in the host country and often prefer no public notice of our visit. When Spanish is spoken, we like to spend time among those who do not speak English in order to practice our only foreign language.

We always try to discourage our hosts from making any special preparations for us, because we realize that our presidential visits often resulted in totally changed places by the time we arrived. Even now, this sometimes happens.

Japan is one of our favorite places to visit. On one of our recent trips in the northwestern region we particularly wanted to learn more about local farming practices, and one of our requests was to see a rice farm that had not been changed very much by mechanization.

With typical Japanese hospitality, our hosts overwhelmed us with their preparations. When we arrived, all the country roads and even the paths between rice paddies had been hastily paved so we wouldn't get our feet dusty. A multicolored tent had been erected at the most advantageous place for us to observe the planting of rice without being exposed to the direct rays of the sun. Four women were in the field planting the green shoots in the traditional way, and the latest tractor-drawn planter was also operating alongside them to demonstrate for us the technological advances of recent years. Along with many news reporters, a hundred or so of the local citizens were assembled near the canopied area to observe our reaction to the scene.

This was not at all what we had had in mind, but we were aware of the tremendous amount of well-meaning work that had gone into the preparations for our visit. There was an uncomfortable few minutes as we tried to adjust to the unexpected conditions. It was Amy who saved the day. She took off her shoes and stockings, tied up her long skirt, and waded out into the knee-deep water where the women were working. After a few moments of stunned silence, the assembled crowd broke into laughter, applause, and then cheers. The farm wives showed her how to plant the rice sprouts in the soft bottom mud, and she worked along with them. The television and still cameras recorded the scene, of course, and Amy was the lead story on the evening TV news and in the next morning's newspapers. A series of human interest stories about her followed during the rest of the week, making Amy something of a hero.

Some months later the Japanese media was fascinated with Amy's arrest for demonstrating against apartheid at the South African embassy in Washington, and she was subsequently invited back to Japan and presented a prestigious humanitarian award, the first foreigner to receive this particular honor.

One of our most interesting trips was a postponement from White House days. The Iranian hostage crisis had prevented a planned presidential visit to China in 1980, after we established diplomatic relations between our two countries, but in 1981 we were able to make the trip as private citizens. We began the tour in Beijing with three days of sightseeing and meetings with the top political leaders, discussing international issues and making arrangements with them to participate in future consultations at the Carter Center.

We made our way—or rather, ate our way—through rounds of almost unbelievable banquets at lunch- and suppertime, with as many as twenty courses of exotic foods and any number of toasts, amid increasingly animated conversation and laughter. Our Chinese hosts always had two sets of chopsticks—one with which to eat and the other to pile additional portions of food on our plates. If we managed, with relief, to get down our first portion of shark's fins and sea slugs, they would quickly slip more onto our plates! In self-defense, we soon learned to reciprocate the courtesy and pile food on our hosts' plates as they drank and laughed. Chip and Amy were along with us on this trip, and one day when we asked Chip if he was having a good time, he said, "Well, I've spent seven hours eating, drinking, talking and laughing already today." He spoke for all of us!

Most Communist countries put some limits on the movement of foreigners, and we had this problem in China, where we were otherwise treated royally. We wanted to see the country as intimately as possible, so shortly after our arrival the first afternoon we requested bicycles for our use while in the capital city. Thus began a subtle minuet with the Chinese security agents. First our guides said there were no bicycles to lend us. We were determined to move around without restraint and told them that we would go out ourselves to rent or purchase enough for our family. Within an hour five bikes were parked in front of the guesthouse.

Early the next morning the chief of security informed us that they had an enjoyable route laid out for us along some of the more rural roads. When we replied that we would rather choose our own itinerary, the chief gave us a map of the city and asked that we mark our proposed path so they could prepare the way.

ROSALYNN

By this time Jimmy was getting impatient and a little angry. When the chief finally told us that it would be impossible for us to choose our route as we went along, Jimmy told him to have someone contact Vice Premier Deng Xiaoping and inform him that because of security restraints we were not being permitted to travel freely, and that we requested his advice.

We went back into the house and the door had hardly closed behind us when there was an urgent knock. We opened it to a smiling chief of security, who said, "Mr. President, you may, of course, go wherever you wish." After the confrontation the guards relaxed, and we had a good time together.

In the cities and in the more remote farming communities we visited the local bakeries and markets, and watched woodworkers, blacksmiths, potters, and other artisans at work. While wandering down unpaved streets or country lanes we were often invited to enter one of the homes for refreshments. Sometimes there would only be half an apple or a cup of hot water, but the welcome would be genuine, and our hosts never apologized for their lack of more elaborate amenities.

On an unannounced visit to a community health center, patients being treated with acupuncture told us of almost miraculous cures of crippling diseases and the alleviation of pain. By strict disciplinary measures, possible only in a totalitarian society, and using intensive educational programs and trained paramedics who work closely with village leaders, the Chinese have reduced their infant mortality rate, carried out a broad immunization program, practically eradicated venereal disease, and lowered the annual population growth rate. Their goal is to reduce the growth rate to zero, using the motto "One is best, two is most."

In a rural community near Xian we joined local anglers alongside a lake, and fished with them for several hours using long bamboo poles, silk lines, and homemade hooks with no eyes. The lines were wrapped around the shank of the hooks and secured with what fly-fishermen call a nail knot. Our bait was tiny balls of dough, and though the bites of the fish were almost undetectable, the fishermen soon taught us how to catch them. We caught three nice carp and took one of them back to the house where we were staying. That evening it was served to us in a bowl of hot milk in which it had been poached. The flesh crumbled easily off the many tiny bones, and we ate the delicious mixture like oyster stew.

During our visit we learned that about 15 percent of the farmland was being cultivated independently by families who were part of the communal agricultural projects in the country, and that most of them also had some kind of small industry within their homes. This was a radical departure from the times of Mao Zedong and the Cultural Revolution. The families we visited either raised chickens, goats, sheep, or mink, made clay pots or small wooden carts, or did repair work on bicycles or other kinds of machinery. They told us they were free to sell their own products and keep the profits after fulfilling their cooperative obligations. We were also told that the farmers' yield is much higher on their own small plots of land than on the communal farms.

During Vice Premier Deng's visit to Washington in 1979 he had shown great interest in our religious beliefs, and we had a long discussion about the role of Christian missionaries in his country. We told him that as small children we used to save pennies for a special offering at Sunday School every week to help educate and feed the children in China. He said that he was an atheist, but acknowledged that many of his nation's schools, hospitals, and universities were begun by Christian missionaries when they were free to work among his people.

JIMMY

> We were sitting at the table during the state dinner, and I finally told him that I had some requests I would like to make. "I hope your people will be permitted to have Bibles and that freedom of religion can be guaranteed for them again. And also, there are a lot of missionaries who would like to return to China to work in education, health care, agriculture, or wherever you would prefer."
>
> Deng thought for a few minutes and then said, "I will consider your first two requests, but we will never again permit foreign religious workers to come to China. They interfere in the daily lives of those they profess to serve, and they also attempt to substitute Western values for those of our people. Even Chinese Christians would not want the foreigners to come back."

Now, in Shanghai more than two years later, we found four large Protestant churches and one even more spacious Catholic cathedral. In conversations with some of the Chinese ministers, we learned that the recent national congress of the Communist party had amended the constitution to guarantee freedom of worship, and that Bibles were now plentiful. "As a matter of fact," said one Chinese Anglican priest, "recently when we ran short of the special paper for Bibles, the government helped us locate and purchase what we needed."

He told us that his church could seat seven hundred and that he had to conduct three morning services to accommodate the crowds, and that the Catholic cathedral celebrated Mass four times each Sunday, with all the pews full. There were still constraints on the expansion of buildings or the construction of new ones. When we offered a contribution to the church, it was refused. "We prefer to be self-sufficient in our work," he said.

Most of our travels have tended to be more directly associated with programs at the center. As part of our work on the Middle East we made an extensive visit to the region in 1983. In addition to our meetings with leaders, we did our best to learn as much as possible about the ordinary daily life, something we couldn't have done as the First Family.

We wandered through Jerusalem at dawn and chatted with people getting ready for the day, going on their way to work or opening their shops. We ate hot fresh bread, right out of stone ovens down below the streets in the old city, and made our way along the Christian Stations of the Cross. At the invitation of the mayor we even jogged around the top of the city wall one morning as the sun rose in the east. It was Purim, a festival commemorating the survival of the Jews in the fifth century B.C., as related in the Old Testament book of Esther, and we laughed with the children on their way to school dressed in costumes for the celebration. We visited places we had never been before in Israel, and spent several days on the West Bank and in the Gaza district among the Christian and Moslem Palestinians.

In Damascus we took time to walk down the "Street called Straight," where Saint Paul had his sight restored after his conversion. We shopped in the outdoor bazaars and saw the holy places. We spent a day with farmers in the countryside, looking at the apricot groves that are their major source of income.

And we paid a call on President Amin Gemayel in Lebanon, where we careened through the streets of Beirut at high speed, surrounded by jeeps loaded with soldiers and U.S. Marines. Our haste could not hide the devastation of war—bombed-out buildings with people still living in them; telltale scenes of soldiers in all kinds of uniforms standing guard at machine-gun stations all along the sidewalks with guns slung over their shoulders; and little children playing all around them, some with miniature weapons of their own, others running their wagons and race cars down tracks cut into the sides of the earthen bunkers.

ROSALYNN

The frantic ride ended at the palace, which had been shelled by gunfire only a few days before. The president and his wife seemed relatively calm as they showed us the damage, which was confined to one small area. Lebanese officials from the different religious and political groups welcomed us at a lovely reception, and then while Jimmy met with some of the leaders I visited with the wives, who talked about the Lebanon that used to be: a beautiful land, with the sea and beaches, the cedars, ideal climate, bountiful fruit and olives and almonds—and peace. Will there ever be peace again in this war-torn country?

We talked with farmers in Jordan and examined the excellent agricultural projects on the East Bank of the river. And then we flew to Petra in the southern mountains, where we approached the ruins of this ancient city through a narrow gorge, with vertical sandstone sides reaching hundreds of feet toward the sky. Though the pass always seemed to be converging ahead of us to a dead end, our Jordanian guides said it was leading us to the Valley of Moses, where the Israelites had miraculously received water when God told Moses to strike a rock with his staff. Whether or not Moses passed this way, the Nabataeans established a fortress city here, known in biblical times as Sela and now as Petra, or sometimes as the "rose-red city."

After a mile or so we rounded a bend, and suddenly before us was the enormous columned façade of a Grecian temple carved in the rose-colored cliff, brilliant in the sunshine. It was breathtaking. We examined the elaborate tombs and caves, some of which are now used as dwellings. It seemed as if many aeons and thousands of miles separated us from the current problems of the Middle East.

On this same trip we cruised slowly up the Nile River for four days, enjoying the calm ride, stopping at the antiquity sites and the villages along the riverbanks. On a Sunday morning we worshiped with Coptics and marveled at their ancient ceremonies, relatively unchanged for nineteen centuries.

From the boat we observed farmers and their families at work in the fertile fields along the river, still plowing with oxen and buffalo, and harvesting crops by hand. Local officials were concerned that many of them were growing forage crops instead of much-needed food grains and products, such as cotton, for export. With artificially depressed grain prices, farmers were abandoning grain crops and concentrating their efforts on products that might be sold for profit at the local markets and were increasingly raising animals for red meat. Some of the farmers told us that they were even taking the cheap imported food grain or bread made from it and using it to feed sheep, goats, and cattle—a terrible waste of protein. In other African countries, similar situations, compounded by years of drought, have discouraged food production. We knew that conditions were especially bad in the neighboring countries of Ethiopia and Sudan.

Although no two nations are completely alike, there is a pattern of change in developing countries that should be of concern to the entire world. With skyrocketing oil prices since 1973, the people in many communities have scavenged the countryside looking for wood, cutting nearby trees, then ranging farther and farther from home to find fuel. Some women and children now spend six or seven hours a day just gathering wood.

When the forests are gone, the soil erodes rapidly, and water that had previously soaked into the land runs off into nearby streams. Famine comes, farmers and others move to the cities, and the country goes further into debt as it imports food and has little to sell to other nations.

As we have traveled through countries in Africa, Asia, and Latin America, we have become more and more familiar with this vicious cycle of poverty, urbanization, and increasing debt. Just paying the interest on foreign loans for many poor countries often requires as much as half the profits from all their exported goods, leaving little income to raise the standard of living of the people.

We pondered what we could do about the problems of hunger in Africa and the foreign-debt crisis in these countries. The partial answer came when Mr. Ryoichi Sasakawa, a Japanese philanthropist, offered to help finance the Global 2000 project in Africa to teach farmers how to increase their food production.

Working with Dr. Borlaug on this, we recruited some of the same agricultural scientists who had been so successful in the earlier but similar projects in India and Pakistan. We chose to begin work in four countries that had suffered severely from famine but still have the potential of increasing their production of food grains—Ghana, Sudan, Tanzania, and Zambia. The leaders of these countries have cooperated fully, agreeing to let the farmers sell their produce at a fair market price. In the Sudan, at our request, the government even made available ten thousand acres of irrigated land on which to grow the special hybrid sorghum seed needed.

We work only with small farmers and planned to begin the first year with about thirty families in each nation scattered widely through the major grain-producing areas, and then to increase the number in subsequent years. Actually, because of the enthusiasm of the host countries, our first year began with more than ten times that number.

In effect, each farm is a miniature demonstration station, showing neighbors the advantages of better farming methods. Working closely with each family, we encourage the use of good seed and an adequate amount of fertilizer, the choice of the best planting dates, proper weed control, and advantageous marketing or farm storage at harvest time. With the help of generous donors, we can make available small farm loans, to be repaid at harvest time. In some countries most of the sorghum and maize is still planted with a pointed stick and cultivated by hand or with a homemade hoe, and we make no attempt to change the level of mechanization. We do not want the neighboring farmers to say, "If I just had one of those little Japanese tractors I could also increase my yield."

JIMMY

My profession before politics was agriculture, specifically the production and processing of seed. This new project is like having a number of farms in several countries, where the potential for increased production is great. Our hope is that these nations might become self-sufficient in food production and even be able to export substantial quantities of grain to their neighbors.

ROSALYNN

Latin America has been special to us for a long time, ever since we went to Mexico the year our oldest child, Jack, graduated from high school. We were having a hard time adjusting to the fact that our firstborn was soon to be leaving home. We wanted to have the whole family together one more time before it happened, so we drove to Mexico and spent three weeks traveling around the country. Whenever possible, we stayed in places where only Spanish was spoken. It was the first time we had ever tried to speak it after studying the language for years, and it was a thrill to make real contact.

We feel an especially strong affinity for the people of Central and South America. They are so open with their affection and their emotions; if they care for you, they let you know it. They are deeply religious and work hard to make a living, sometimes under primitive conditions. Many of them live in poverty, having been exploited by their own governments and by wealthy nations that have plundered their countries' rich natural resources. But they are always warm, always friendly, and they have a good time!

Latin America has been a focus of our studies at the Carter Center, and we have traveled there several times since we left the White House. Peru had become a democracy while Jimmy was still in office, and I went to the inauguration of their newly elected president. I wanted to visit Machu Picchu then, but canceled my plans when I learned that our government would have to fly American helicopters all the way to Peru to take me to that remote mountain area. When we visited in 1985 we were able to make the trip through the courtesy of the Peruvian Air Force.

Machu Picchu is an ancient fortress city of the Incas in the Andes Mountains, one of the few pre-Columbian urban centers found nearly intact. The site, on a low peak and sheltered by high mountains, includes a temple and a citadel that were once surrounded by terraced gardens linked by more than three thousand steps. And we climbed most of them! At an altitude of about eighty-five hundred feet, that was no small achievement.

We like to visit Habitat projects on our overseas trips, often traveling far from the major cities to meet the local people and give encouragement to our American volunteers. In Peru our major housing projects are in the southern high plains region near Lake Titicaca. The day after we went to Machu Picchu we visited one of them at Puno, being built at an altitude of thirteen thousand feet. These are some of our most expensive overseas homes, costing about three thousand U.S. dollars. Much of the building materials have to be hauled in because there are no trees at that altitude, and the local clays are not suitable for homemade bricks and roofing tile.

ROSALYNN

Later on that same trip we went to Brazil. When our plane arrived in Rio, which to me is one of the most beautiful cities in the world, we were met by Governor Leonel Brizzola and two of his grandchildren. The children greeted us with bouquets of red roses and words of welcome, but the governor was speechless. He clasped Jimmy to him, but couldn't utter a word.

We walked into the airport, chatting with the children to make their grandfather feel more at ease. A press conference had been set up, and the governor began to speak: "I wanted you here because I have a story to tell. During the time this man was president, I was forced to live in exile in Uruguay because my government considered me to be a dangerous political adversary. One day I had a call from officials in that country saying that I was being sent back home, which meant for me certain imprisonment, if not execution. I didn't know what I was going to do.

"That same day, I was driving past the American embassy. On the spur of the moment, I decided to stop and see if there was anything to this human rights policy of the United States that I had been hearing about. I began to tell the Americans my story and discovered that they already knew about me. When they learned that I was being deported, they said, 'Let us see what we can do.' It was a Friday afternoon, and they asked me to come back on Monday. But on Monday my house was surrounded by soldiers. I called to tell them that I was under the authority of guards who would not permit me to leave my home. Their answer to me was, 'We have contacted Washington and as of this moment you are under the authority of the president of the United States.'"

With the agreement of the Uruguayan leaders, he was brought to the United States with his family. Later, after a change in the government of Brazil, he returned to his homeland and was soon elected governor of Rio. When he finished his story, there was hardly a dry eye in the crowd.

We ended our Latin American journey in Mexico and came away with increased concern about this and other countries whose debt loads are staggering and who are facing crises for which no solutions are evident.

Regardless of the purpose of going somewhere, we get real pleasure from anticipating the trip and reading extensively about the places we are going to see. Information is available to anyone who wants it; there are many sources, including tourist bureaus, the U.S. State Department, and local libraries. The material can provide new ideas on what to do and offers incentives to get off the tourist beats of big hotels, organized bus tours, large cities, and Western-style resorts.

We have met many Americans who are pursuing hobbies overseas: hunting and fishing, golfing, biking, studying music and art, examining European cathedral architecture, hang gliding or soaring, and mountain climbing. There is a natural tie of friendship and camaraderie with others who enjoy the same pastimes, and often families or clubs with similar interests are glad to be hosts in foreign lands, which is also a way of curbing costs.

On a mountain peak overlooking St. Moritz in Switzerland we

recently talked to a retired couple who travel extensively as members of a photography club in Tennessee. Traveling in small groups to interesting and photogenic places, they share the more advanced techniques of their hobby with local photographers and give slide presentations at schools and at civic and social clubs when they return home.

Modern jet travel has made it possible for Americans of average income to participate for two to four weeks in fact-finding and travel seminars in all parts of the world, especially in troubled regions. Both religious and nonsectarian organizations arrange for small groups to participate in discussions with politicians, opposition leaders, dissidents, newspaper editors, academics, and ordinary people to gain a better understanding of conditions and issues. These discussions offer a considerably deeper look at areas in the Middle East or countries like Nicaragua or Guatemala than would otherwise be feasible. Some professional organizations provide special tours as well.

A Presbyterian group was in the Philippines not long after President Corazon Aquino came to power, and others have been to the Soviet Union and Southeast Asia. Another group met Jews, Christians, and Muslims in Jerusalem and participated in a work project in Egypt. They call this program Global Awareness Through Experience (GATE). The participants enjoy sightseeing, but their main emphasis is to learn as much as possible about their host country and to determine what, if anything, they can do to alleviate some of the problems.

A Lutheran group recently spent three weeks in the Middle East learning about Orthodox and Coptic Christians and their relationship to Islam, while others went to Africa and the island nations in the Pacific.

The Citizens Exchange Council, a nonsectarian, nonpolitical organization, offers travel seminars to the Soviet Union and Eastern Europe for small groups with similar vocations or interests—photographers, teachers, writers, artists, musicians. Participants visit collective farms, hospitals, schools, and performing-arts workshops, and join in other activities the average tourist would never seek, both in large cities and more out-of-the-way places, meeting with Soviet and other foreign citizens with similar interests.

These kinds of trips reflect not only the greater mobility possible in the latter part of the twentieth century, as distances that once took months can be covered in hours, but also a growing sense of responsibility toward actively working for peace and brotherhood through individual and group understanding. In the space of a vacation period, participants gain a much deeper look at sensitive areas than would be possible for most persons traveling on their own.

In October 1985 we made a two-week visit to Nepal. What an adventure it was! This is the only Hindu kingdom in the world, with a strong Buddhist minority, mostly in the mountains. There is a remarkable geographical diversity here, ranging from lowland plains to the world's highest peaks. Kathmandu, the capital, is in a beautiful valley that is really a huge outdoor museum. We were primarily interested in hiking in the Himalayas, but also learned a lot about the country and its people.

We visited homes and schools for children of parents suffering from leprosy. We included a visit with the Christian missionaries in the country, who work among the poor but are not allowed to proselytize, and got to know a number of the young Peace Corps volunteers, most of whom work in small, remote villages. Near the end of our visit we enjoyed an evening with the young king, Birendra Bir Bikram Shah, and his family, and had an extended lunch with the members of the cabinet. This gave us a chance to review with them some of our experiences, to get answers to many questions, and to deliver a few requests we had picked up along the way from Nepalese people concerning such things as the need for electric power and the repair of trails that had been washed away.

JIMMY

Trekking in the mountains was the most strenuous exercise of our lives, but I found it exhilarating. Because of delays caused by unseasonable rains in the lowlands and deep new-fallen snow in the mountains, we had to begin at what would have been the midpoint of our trek. The abbreviated schedule was obviously too ambitious. A number of the party had to be evacuated from the high mountains by helicopter because of exhaustion and altitude sickness. Rosalynn stayed with us until the next to last day, reaching 15,000 feet before she turned back to Pheriche, the nearest village.

A few in our party made it to a cliff above the Everest Base Camp and some of us decided to climb even higher than we had originally planned. We could see the peak called Kala Pattar, or Black Pinnacle, above us. Although we had no crampons or even a rope, we began the ascent, clinging to rocks that often moved as we grasped them. The snow and a coating of ice made every foothold uncertain, and it took two hours to make the relatively short climb. When I reached the pinnacle, my pleasure at our accomplishment was not as strong as my anger at myself for being so foolhardy. Knowing nothing about the technical aspects of mountain climbing and ill equipped for such a steep climb, I had taxed my endurance and ability almost beyond their limits.

We were 18,500 feet above sea level, with many hours of often treacherous walking, most of it during the night, before we could get back to Pheriche. I realized that determination and willingness to accept discomfort to achieve a goal could easily become dangerous in this land of exquisite beauty and awesome challenges. We were lucky, in that none of us suffered any lasting ill effects.

ROSALYNN

This story has to be told in two versions, since Jimmy and I had such differing impressions of the trip. He was healthy and exuberant during the whole time, to the chagrin of most of us who got tired, cold, and wet, and, at certain points, miserable. He got tired, cold, and wet, too, but he never had any reaction to the altitude, and the beauty of the mountains and the adventure of the trip made his adrenaline flow. Only he and two others in our party felt good all of the time and made it to the top of Kala Pattar.

We made plans for our trip to Nepal for over a year, and everyone we spoke to about it was envious. We read books, studied maps, and had sessions with our traveling companions to decide on trekking routes. We bought jackets and down pants that zipped over our jeans to keep us warm during the nights that were going to be cold. We carefully made lists of the things we would need to take with us—flashlights, trail mix, Granola bars, aspirin, soap. Someone suggested sponges to bathe with instead of washcloths—it was a good idea—toilet paper, sunscreen, hat, powdered Gatorade, lipstick and zinc oxide for our lips when we reached the bright snow. We collected our supplies for months in advance, remembering that we would have to carry our backpacks and could have only one small bag in addition.

The day finally arrived when we were on our way. Kathmandu was fascinating. We wandered through the streets, observing the rituals of the Hindu and Buddhist worshipers, the ancient temples and monasteries, the pigeons and goats roosting and clambering over the idols, people hawking their wares. But we had only one night to take it all in, so anxious were we to get on to the mountains and our trekking adventure.

And then the weather didn't cooperate. We boarded a large helicopter to fly to the base of a mountain range on the west side of the country where our trek would begin in the low altitudes. The fog was so dense that we couldn't see anything, and already I was beginning to have doubts. How many mountains were out there, and did the pilot really know where we were? This was not the United States with instruments and radar beams to guide a craft onto a landing strip. Finally, after almost an hour when we could see nothing through the "soup," the clouds lifted for a moment and there below was a small airport—and we landed. It wasn't close to where we were going; but we weren't going anywhere else. No sooner had we touched down than the clouds closed in again and we were stranded.

It was an adventure, all right, from beginning to end. We never did make it into the low mountains where we were supposed to trek for a week, up to altitudes of around nine thousand feet. The rains continued, with heavy fog. Higher in the mountains the rains turned to snow, and several trekking parties were trapped. Rescue efforts were necessary during the next few days.

We finally flew to Namche Bazar in the Everest area on the east side of the country, and began what was supposed to be the second week of our trek—at twelve thousand feet!

The first day we didn't try to climb any higher, but walked for five hours, slowly, to a village at the same altitude. That's not to say the terrain was level. It was up and down, up and down—down into the valleys and up again over the next mountains. We walked on trails made by yaks and mountain goats and other travelers. In one place an avalanche had sent water rushing down the valley, washing out the sides of the mountain so that the narrow path on the ledge that we were following had slipped into the valley. We managed to wind our way down to the floor of the chasm, and at a point where a footbridge had once been we climbed on rocks and a few logs over the rushing mountain waters. And this time when we finally made our ascent up the other side of the chasm, sometimes on our hands and knees, there in the distance was a beautiful sight—our campsite for the night!

When we reached our tent I fell into it—I have never been so tired in all my life. There was not a mountain peak in sight, though we were told that they were all around us, rising to towering heights. But the sky had been overcast for most of the day, and everything was damp and gray.

I had just begun to relax, sprawled out on the mat on the floor of the tent, when Jimmy stuck his head in and said, "Come on. There's a *gompa* [Buddhist monastery] just at the top of that ridge. Let's go see it." I don't know why I got up. I didn't think I could move, but I did. I crawled out of the low opening of the tent, and put one foot in front of the other. Jimmy promised that he would walk at my speed, and everybody else in the party gave a sigh of relief.

We made our way up the mountainside, and just at the last turn on the zigzag road to the *gompa*, nestled under a clump of trees, were two of the most beautiful birds I had ever seen. Our sherpa guide said they were blood pheasants. We admired them and moved on. We had gone only a short distance when suddenly another pair of large birds flew off a ledge right over my head. Getting out of their way, I almost fell down, but looked up in time to catch a glimpse of the impeyan pheasants, or *danphe*. The rare national bird of Nepal, the *danphe* is brilliant, with nine bright colors—if possible, even more beautiful than the blood pheasant.

We reached our destination, and learned that the head lama was in Namche Bazar, the village we had left early in the morning! But we wandered through the monastery, soaking in the quietness, the history, the spirit of the place in this secluded, ancient, seemingly forgotten spot where for centuries people have worshiped their gods and lived in peace.

We had just left and begun our descent to the village when someone cried, "Look, look up there!" We looked, and it was as though the heavens had opened up. There in full view, as through a window in the clouds, was a mountain peak covered with snow, brilliant in the sunshine. Just as quickly as it had appeared, it was gone. But seeing it was worth all the long, hard climb of the day. It was magnificent, as magnificent as the mountains we would be viewing for the remainder of our trip. The birds, the glimpse of the mountain, the hot meal that was waiting for us, the warmth of the sleeping bag, all combined to let me know that this trip would be special.

It was special, but it was hard—hard, taxing, demanding of physical energy. It was not always fun. I didn't always feel good. I wanted to go home at times. I wanted to eat my cooking at times. I wanted to be through with it before it was done.

But the memories linger—of the beauty and grandeur of the mountains, of the moon at night rising over them so that everything is golden in the first light and then silver as it climbs higher. I remember with special fondness the sherpas who walked with us, carrying our supplies, giving a helpful hand when a foot slipped on a rock, or walking on the edge of the cliff between me and the drop-off so I would feel safer, pouring us a cup of hot lemon tea every time we paused to catch our breath, or filling our water bottles with hot water at night to put in our sleeping bag to keep our feet warm. They were wonderful, and they were as much at home on these mountains as were the mountain goats. Some of them were children and relatives of our head sherpa, and the young girls that looked after me were in their teens.

I have memories of prayer wheels, large and small, which spin prayers up to heaven, and of prayer flags that flap their messages to the gods and by whose numbers let us know how dangerous were the shaky footbridges that we sometimes had to cross. I remember walking around the left side of the Buddhist prayer offerings—sometimes one

large rock, sometimes enormous piles of individual prayer stones—
when often it meant a steep ascent rather than a more level path, just
to please the sherpas who were too devout to approve of walking
counterclockwise around the shrines. I can still see the yaks being
herded along the narrow paths, with tinkling bells around their necks,
and children in the occasional village in the lower altitudes, with runny
noses and chapped skin, bundled in warm clothes that they must
never take off, and their smiling faces as they saw the bubbles they
blew from the bottle of soapsuds I had in my backpack. And I
remember the beauty of an outhouse, even one over just a hole in the
ground, but at least with sides!

Will I go back? Time will tell. Right now, I really don't know—but
I'm glad I've already been.

We do a lot of traveling, but we have to be careful about the costs.
As a result we have done what we could to enable others to enjoy
people-to-people visits with maximum benefit and minimum cost. This
is one reason we have been so eager to help with the Friendship Force
program.

In working with Wayne Smith, our earliest exchanges between
Georgia and Pernambuco, Brazil, were somewhat experimental. But
they led to lasting friendships and goodwill between the people of two
different countries.

ROSALYNN

I went on the first trip of this exchange program and stayed with a
family that I came to love. They live on a beautiful beach in
Pernambuco. The husband owns a small business and his wife is originally from Colorado. I have been back several times to see them, they
have been to visit us, and their daughter came to Atlanta one year to
be the international queen of our annual dogwood festival.

They happen often now, these visits back and forth, between
Friendship Force "ambassadors." My mother, at age seventy-two,
participated in an exchange between Georgia and Newcastle, England.

She still corresponds with her hosts there, and they have been to Plains to visit her.

The Friendship Force is now reaching into parts of the world that we couldn't have imagined when it was originally conceived. And friendships are being made that can only lead to a more peaceful world. Even in countries such as Poland and China where we have not yet been able to arrange overnight visits in private homes, Friendship Force ambassadors are enjoying "home hospitality"—meals and weekend outings with local families—in lieu of "home stays." Our newest program is one with the Soviet Union that has been named American-Russian Mutual Survival, or ARMS, by Wayne Smith. It is his belief that we should use arms to embrace, rather than for war. Our aim is to take one hundred people from each state to the Soviet Union every year and bring the same number of Russians to this country. We have already signed an agreement with Soviet officials to that effect. For the first time, citizens of both countries are being permitted to visit in private homes and to travel with relative freedom around the host communities.

When the first group of thirty visitors came from Soviet Georgia to visit our Georgia, we joined them on Sunday for church and an outdoor picnic. Wayne lives in a mountain development a few miles from our log cabin and preaches in a little chapel there when he is at home. That Sunday all the Russians were in church, including a quartet who sang our regular Christian songs with the choir and then provided an impressive medley of classical songs. During the service different members of the Soviet delegation were called on to speak, and each said that though we have different languages, there is room for friendship and peaceful coexistence. The very conservative residents of this north Georgia community listened intently to the interpreter, and, when the speeches were over, spontaneously rose to their feet in a standing ovation.

ROSALYNN

In 1984 we visited Hiroshima, where Jimmy made a speech at "ground zero" to several thousand people. He spoke about the suffering that had taken place at Pearl Harbor and here where the first nuclear bomb had been dropped, and warned of the worldwide holocaust that would result if nations could not find better ways to settle their differences than through war. Later, officials of the city informed us that they were planning a Friendship Force exchange—between citizens of Hiroshima and Pearl Harbor.

We have learned through this program that everyone can contribute to better international understanding. A friendly smile, a warm hello, can help break down barriers that sometimes separate us from those who are different.

You don't have to go far from home to have interesting travel experiences. Many people in Plains belong to the Thirty-Niners Club. This private group organizes bus tours for its members to various spots in the United States and Canada, and, as one of the members said, "makes it possible for me to travel because it is inexpensive."

Anyone can join the club, although most of the travelers are older, with only one trip each year being planned for children and grandchildren. Membership in the club has now reached fifteen thousand, with participants in all fifty states. The calendar of events for 1986 showed trips to Washington, D.C., to the Rose Bowl in Los Angeles by way of Carlsbad Caverns and the Grand Canyon, to New England for a fall foliage tour, and a spring tulip trip through Niagara Falls and into Canada.

ROSALYNN

My mother has been on two of these trips with a group of her friends, and enjoyed each one immensely. On the first trip her group flew to Hawaii. A bus was waiting for them at the airport, "with a Hawaiian guide," she said, "and all our accommodations were already arranged." They toured the islands every day and saw the sights. The other was a brief trip to shop at several big discount houses in South Carolina, and then to see the "spectacular" (her word) Christmas lights in

McAddenville, North Carolina, and the American Heritage Village in Charlotte. When I asked her if she didn't get very tired, she said, "No, it's a great thing. I want to go on the tulip tour into Canada next year."

Allan Fromme says, "It is remarkable how a trip, despite all its inconveniences, can freshen our point of view. A change in routine, a new scene, can help us become more alive again. But we really needn't go to the expense of travel to accomplish the same thing. There are almost always unfamiliar parts of town to explore, new foods to taste, different news programs and papers to try, dozens of innovative ways to make tomorrow different."*

So whether we are looking for pleasure, adventure, or a way to expand our business and professional lives, to become better educated, or to contribute to the well-being of others, travel can help us make the most of the rest of our lives.

---

*Allan Fromme, *Life after Work* (Glenview, Ill.: Scott, Foresman & Co., 1984).

Winding Up

When you're pushing sixty, that's exercise enough.

—Jimmy Townsend

Not long ago we noticed a mobile camper just in front of us as we came up to the traffic light in Plains. A carefully painted sign on the back said, "We canceled our will and bought this van. Our kids know we're enjoying life."

As we approach retirement age it is natural to have more frequent and somber thoughts about the end of our lives, although all the great religions teach us not to fear death. But perhaps it is even more important not to be afraid of advancing age. This late period can be a time of foreboding and resignation, a time merely of assessment and contemplation. But it also offers the chance to be bolder than ever before and to do worthwhile things that have been avoided or postponed for five or six decades. To take that chance is what this book is really meant to encourage.

Retirement can be one of life's greatest dangers if all we do is brace ourselves to face what we think will be many barren and useless years. At worst, there are some who lose the will to live, especially those who have been very ambitious or productive in earlier years. They fear a monotonous life without purpose—and without respect from others. But this need not happen.

As we have tried to show, longer life and earlier retirement can create significant new opportunities. A second career can be gratifying because it is built upon many years of experience, accumulated knowledge, influence, and perhaps freedom from financial uncertainty. This period may offer the first chance to repay our community by service and sharing, for which there had previously never been the time. This career also warrants as much careful thought and planning as we gave our first one.

JIMMY

> Since I was a young boy the thrust of my prayers—at least when I was trying to make a good impression on God—has always been that I not fail to use fully and effectively the one life I have on earth. I have always enjoyed difficult challenges. At the same time I have faced the realization that it is not easy to take a chance or confront the prospect of failure and embarrassment. But my feeling is that if we refuse to try something that might fail, we lack faith either in ourselves or in our causes and goals.

It is often more convenient to back off and cling to one's own suspected shortcomings or the lack of a nearly perfect opportunity as a convenient excuse to do nothing. One of the most revealing discussions at our "Closing the Gap" conference dealt with people who are prone to mental and physical suffering far beyond what might normally be expected in the context of the real circumstances of their lives. The conclusion drawn was that they have a negative view of their fate, and do not have the will to deal with the vicissitudes of life. They are convinced that what they think or do will not make any difference. This attitude seems to make them more susceptible to mental illness, alcoholism, contagious diseases, accidents, physical abuse, unwanted pregnancy, drug addiction, or even to the temptation of committing criminal acts. To some degree and under some circumstances all of us will choose to "take the easy way out." Neither we nor anyone else can claim to have absolute fortitude. We all stumble.

We need a sense of control over our lives if we are to avoid being resigned to defeat or failure. It is necessary to recognize the inevitability of disappointment, problems, and failures, and to believe that we are capable of either surmounting or surviving them. We need to be confident that a full and enjoyable life with its share of successes is possible if we are willing to meet the challenges head-on. Arnold Toynbee's *A Study of History* has been in our home library ever since our early navy days, and many times we have been reminded of his basic premise that nations (and people) thrive only when they are contending with crises or challenges.

At any time in life, it is appropriate to ponder the question "For me, what is success?" With a number of major changes in our lives, we have found it necessary to consider the question on numerous occasions. It has not always been easy to find the right answer.

In a recent Sunday School discussion we talked about what we might do that would enable us to experience a sense of joy and peace in times of adversity. There was general agreement that we should inventory our talents and interests, that our goals in life should be worthy as measured by God, that we should attempt things that might be beyond our abilities, and that this would put us in a spirit of submission to God's will. Once we do all this, we can then undertake worthy goals with boldness and confidence, realizing that these revised ambitions might be quite different from the more self-serving achievements we had previously coveted.

One of the most valuable lessons we have learned over the years is how much our everyday decisions affect our long-term health and happiness. There is a great temptation while we are in the thick of things to postpone doing what we would either like to do or ought to do: "Maybe next year . . . When we make the last car payment . . . When I retire . . ."

Sometimes we wonder how people like our mothers and Esther Peterson managed to remain so youthful despite their years. All of them had known their share of losses, were widowed, and moved out of their former work in various ways. Yet each of them managed somehow to retain or recapture that youthful ability to move on beyond the discouragement and pain, to enjoy the small victories and laugh at the absurdities along the way. They continued to set new goals, just as small children attempt to learn new tasks. They also kept the same sense of fun and excitement, and were still young at the age of eighty. Other people are already old at eighteen, with their hearts and minds no longer expanding. They are unlikely ever to have ideals or ambitions that amount to very much.

We all have limitations and have to live with them. These can be disappointments in one's first choice of a job or profession, or the much more serious suffering from some severe physical or mental affliction. However, if we are able to make clear assessments of our remaining opportunities with some degree of objectivity, there is a lot we can do to enrich our lives and probably other people's as well. This is all easier said than done, but just knowing that everyone else has limitations and disappointments helps make it easier for us to live with our own. And there is no doubt that setting off on new initiatives can make life invigorating.

In today's world, with the breaking up of the extended family and the urbanization of our society, we have become more isolated, more impersonal in our relationships, and perhaps less sensitive to the needs or pain of others. Loneliness may well be the most striking condition of modern life, but it can be alleviated in various ways.

It takes a deliberate effort to invest wisely any part of our lives to help others. But the effort is worthwhile because when we think we are making the maximum sacrifice we almost invariably derive the greatest blessing.

As we've stressed before, we can also add vitality to our lives by actively experimenting with new interests, tasks, and hobbies. Over the years we ourselves have tried photography, woodworking, gardening, gourmet cooking, fly-fishing, oil painting, bird-watching, collecting old bottles and Indian artifacts, building houses, writing books, and a wide range of sports—cross-country and Alpine skiing, tennis, jogging, bowling, mountain trekking, windsurfing, and biking.

JIMMY

I particularly enjoy reading about all these activities. We make new friends by sharing our interests with others, especially those who have mastered the techniques. If I read a good book about woodworking or fly-fishing, I try to make a point of meeting the author personally.

On a more practical level, we find it satisfying not only to do a lot of our own yard work and most of the repairs and renovations in our home but also to design and build cabinets and furniture, lay a new hardwood floor, do rudimentary plumbing and masonry jobs, and rewire the hi-fi sound system. Also, we are frequently in our woods and fields, either exploring, hunting arrowheads, checking the condition of crops, or assessing the management of forests. We have two farm ponds that provide not only some good fishing but also take some of our time in managing them. All these different tasks provide welcome breaks from the conferences and activities of the Carter Center, correspondence, fund-raising, bookkeeping, telephone calls, university teaching, and writing that require most of our time.

It's probably inevitable that at some point readers of this book will say, "Oh well, sure. Anything is possible for former presidents." But as we've tried to show, there have been times when that made matters worse, not easier. The notion we want to stress is that much of what we've done outside politics is available to almost anyone.

For us, an involvement in promoting good for others has made a tremendous difference in our lives in recent years. There are serious needs everywhere for volunteers who want to help those who are hungry, homeless, blind, crippled, addicted to drugs or alcohol, illiterate, mentally ill, elderly, imprisoned, or just friendless and lonely. For most of us, learning about these people, who are often our immediate neighbors, can add a profound new dimension to what might otherwise be a time of too much worrying about our own selves.

We've said that our early lives, our families, and surroundings helped to shape not only our habits and attitudes but also our subsequent commitments. On a farm or in a small rural community during the Depression years, it was impossible to live a life of isolation from our neighbors. We shared almost everything, including a lot of knowledge about specific skills. For example, if something was broken, we usually had to fix it ourselves. With time off from work, we also shared sports, games, hunting, fishing, and the visits of friends and relatives. Much of what we do now comes from that background.

Since leaving the White House we have had a chance to revive a number of our old interests and pursue some new ones, a process that we hope will continue for the rest of our lives. There is no way to know how many years we will have to spend together, and we want to make the most of them. In addition to having a good time, we have taken on some challenging projects, but our tendency has been to move toward the simpler activities that we can share with each other and our friends—and enjoy now and for a long time to come.

Organizations Mentioned in This Book

All addresses and phone numbers listed here have been updated for this 1995 reprint edition of *Everything to Gain*.

Alcoholics Anonymous World
Services
Grand Central Station
P.0. Box 459
New York, NY 10163
(212) 870-3400

American Association of Retired
Persons
601 E Street NW
Washington, DC 20049
(202) 434-2277

American Baptist International
Ministries
P.O. Box 851
Valley Forge, PA 19482
(610) 768-2000

American Red Cross
2025 E Street NW
Washington, DC 20006
(202) 728-6400

Amnesty International, USA
322 Eighth Avenue
New York, NY 10001
(212) 807-8400

Animal Land
c/o Tom T. Hall
Fox Hollow
Franklin, TN 37064

Camp Sunshine
P.O. Box 77236
Atlanta, GA 30309
(404) 872-6977

CARE
151 Ellis Street
Atlanta, GA 30303
(404) 681-2552

Chicago Foundation for Women
230 W. Superior
Suite 400
Chicago, IL 60610
(312) 266-1176

Christmas International House
P.O. Box 764
Tucker, GA 30085-0764
(770) 938-4291

Citizens Exchange Council
12 W. 31st Street
New York, NY 10001
(212) 643-1985

Elderhostel, Inc.
75 Federal Street
Boston, MA 02110-1941
(617) 426-7788

65 Family Focus
1942 Dempster Street
Evanston, IL 60202
(708) 869-1800

Family Focus/Lawndale
3600 W. Ogdan Avenue
Chicago, IL 60623
(312) 521-3306

The Friendship Force
Forsyth Street NW
Suite 900
Atlanta, GA 30303
(404) 522-9490

Habitat for Humanity
121 Habitat Street
Americus, GA 31709
(912) 924-6935

International Executive Service
Corps
333 Ludlow Street
Stamford, CT 06902
(203) 967-6000

International Red Cross
17 Avenue de la Paix
CH-12ll
Geneva, Switzerland

Koinonia Partners
1324 Hwy. 49 South
Americus, GA 31709
(912) 924-0391

Lawyers Committee for Human
Rights
330 7th Avenue
10th Floor
New York, NY 10001
(212) 629-6170

Evangelical Lutheran Church in
America
8765 W. Higgins Road
Chicago, IL 60631
1-800-638-3522

International Executive Service
Corps
333 Ludlow Street
Stamford, CT 06902
(203) 967-6000

Mennonite Mission Board (U.S.)
Box 370
Elkhart, IN 46515-0370
(219) 294-1523

Mennonite Central Committee
(overseas)
P.O. Box 500
Akron, PA 17501
(717) 859-1151

Mennonite Voluntary Service (U.S. and Canada)
General Conference Mennonite Church
722 Main Street
Newton, KS 67114
(316) 283-5100

National Alliance for Research on Schizophrenia and Depression
60 Cutter Mill Road
Suite 200
Great Neck, NY 11021
(516) 829-0091

National Alliance for the Mentally Ill
200 N. Glebe Road
Suite 1015
Arlington, VA 22203-3754
(703) 524-7600

National Conference of Catholic Charities
3311 4th Street NE
Washington, DC 20017
(202) 541-3000

National Depressive and Manic Depressive Assn.
730 N. Franklin
Suite 501
Chicago, IL 60610
(312) 642-0049

National Institute of Mental Health
5600 Fishers Lane
Rockville, MD 20857
(301) 443-4515

(A national clearing house for mental health information is maintained by the NIMH.)

National Executive Service Corps
257 Park Avenue South
2d Floor
New York, NY 10010
(212) 529-6660

National Mental Health Association
1021 Prince Street
Alexandria, VA 22314
(703) 684-1722

The Nature Conservancy
1815 N. Lynn Street
Arlington, VA 22209
(703) 841-5300

Oxfam America
26 West Street
Boston, MA 02111-1206
(617) 482-1211

Partners of the Americas, National Association
1424 K Street NW
Suite 700
Washington, DC 20005
(202) 628-3300

Peace Corps
1990 K Street NW
Washington, DC 20526
(202) 606-3886

Presbyterian Church U.S.A.
Volunteers in Mission
475 Riverside Drive
Suite 240
New York, NY 10115
(212) 870-2221

Presbyterian Church U.S.A.
General Assembly Mission Board
100 Witherspoon Street
Louisville, KY 40204
(502) 569-5000

Prison Fellowship Ministries
P.O. Box 17500
Washington, DC 20041-0500
(703) 478-0100

Southern Baptist Convention
Foreign Mission Board Volunteer
Department
Box 6767
Richmond, VA 23230
(804) 353-0151

Southern Baptist Home Mission
Board
1350 Spring Street NW
Atlanta, GA 30367
(404) 898-7000

Special Olympics
1325 G Street NW
Washington, DC 20005
(202) 628-3630

The Task Force for Child Survival
and Development
One Copenhill
Atlanta, GA 30307
(404) 872-4122

U.S. Committee for the United
Nations Children's Fund
333 East 38th Street
6th Floor
New York, NY 10016
(212) 686-5522

Westville
P.O. Box 1850
Lumpkin, GA 31815
(912) 838-6310